STAAR Grade 8 Math Practice Workbook

2023 – 2024

The Most Comprehensive Review for the Math Section of the STAAR Grade 8 Test

By

Reza Nazari

All inquiries should be addressed to:
info@effortlessMath.com
www.EffortlessMath.com

ISBN: 978-1-63719-045-6

Published by: **Effortless Math Education Inc.**

For Online Math Practice Visit www.EffortlessMath.com

Welcome to
STAAR Grade 8 Math Prep
2023

Thank you for choosing Effortless Math for your STAAR Grade 8 Math test preparation and congratulations on making the decision to prepare for the STAAR Grade 8 test! It's a remarkable move you are taking, one that shouldn't be diminished in any capacity.

That's why you need to use every tool possible to ensure you succeed on the test with the highest possible score, and this extensive math

If math has never been a strong subject for you, don't worry! This book along with our online STAAR Math resources will help you prepare for (and even ACE) the STAAR Grade 8 Math test. As test day draws nearer, effective preparation becomes increasingly more important. Thankfully, you have this comprehensive workbook to help you get ready for the test. With this book and Effortless Math online resources, you can feel confident that you will be more than ready for the STAAR Grade 8 Math test when the time comes.

First and foremost, it is important to note that this book is a workbook and not a textbook. Every lesson of this practice book was carefully developed to ensure that you are making the most effective use of your time while preparing for the test. This up-to-date book reflects the 2023 test guidelines and will put you on the right track to hone your math skills, overcome exam anxiety, and boost your confidence, so that you can have your best to succeed on the STAAR Grade 8 Math test.

This exercise book will:

☑ Explain the format of the STAAR Grade 8 Math test.

☑ Describe specific test-taking strategies that you can use on the test.

☑ Provide STAAR Math test-taking tips.

☑ Help you identify the areas in which you need to concentrate your study time.

☑ Offer exercises that help you develop the basic math skills you will learn in each section.

☑ Give **2 realistic and full-length practice tests** (featuring new question types) with detailed answers to help you measure your exam readiness and build confidence.

This resource contains comprehensive practice questions and exercises that you will need to prepare for the STAAR Grade 8 Math test. You'll get numerous skill building exercises as well as tips and techniques on how to prepare for your STAAR Grade 8 Math test.

In addition, in the following pages you'll find:

➢ **How to Use This Book Effectively** – This section provides you with step-by-step instructions on how to get the most out of this comprehensive study guide.

➢ **How to study for the STAAR Grade 8 Math Test** – A six-step study program has been developed to help you make the best use of this book and prepare for your STAAR Math test. Here you'll find tips and strategies to guide your study program and help you understand STAAR Grade 8 Math and how to ace the test.

➢ **STAAR Grade 8 Math Review** – Learn everything you need to know about the STAAR Grade 8 Math test.

➢ **STAAR Grade 8 Math Test-Taking Strategies** – Learn how to effectively put these recommended test-taking techniques into use for improving your STAAR Grade 8 Math score.

➢ **Test Day Tips** – Review these tips to make sure you will do your best when the big day comes.

Effortless Math's STAAR Grade 8 Online Center

Effortless Math Online STAAR Grade 8 Center offers a complete study program, including the following:

✓ Step-by-step instructions on how to prepare for the STAAR Grade 8 Math test

✓ Numerous STAAR Grade 8 Math worksheets to help you measure your math skills

✓ Complete list of STAAR Grade 8 Math formulas

✓ Video lessons for all STAAR Grade 8 Math topics

✓ Full-length STAAR Grade 8 Math practice tests

✓ And much more…

No Registration Required.

Visit **EffortlessMath.com/STAAR** to find your online STAAR Grade 8 Math resources.

How to Use This Book Effectively

Look no further when you need a study program to improve your math skills to succeed on the math portion of the STAAR Grade 8 test. Each chapter of this comprehensive workbook will provide you with the knowledge, tools, and understanding needed for every topic covered on the test.

It's imperative that you understand each topic before moving onto another one, as that's the way to guarantee your success. You can use Effortless Math online course (a free course) to find examples and a step-by-step guide of every math concept in this workbook to better understand the content that will be on the test. To get the best possible results from this book:

> **Begin studying long before your test date**. This provides you ample time to learn the different math concepts. The earlier you begin studying for the test, the sharper your skills will be. Do not procrastinate! Provide yourself with plenty of time to learn the concepts and feel comfortable that you understand them when your test date arrives.

> **Practice consistently**. Study STAAR Math concepts at least 20 to 30 minutes a day. Remember, slow and steady wins the race, which can be applied to preparing for the STAAR Math test. Instead of cramming to tackle everything at once, be patient and learn the math topics in short bursts.

> Whenever you get a math problem wrong, **mark it off, and review it later** to make sure you understand the concept.

> Start each session by **looking over the previous material.**

> Once you've reviewed the book's exercises, **take a practice test at the back of the book** to gauge your level of readiness. Then, review your results. Read detailed answers and solutions for each question you missed.

> **Take another practice test** to get an idea of how ready you are to take the actual exam. Taking the practice tests will give you the confidence you need on test day. Simulate the STAAR testing environment by sitting in a quiet room free from distraction. Make sure to clock yourself with a timer.

How to Study for the STAAR Grade 8 Math Test

Studying for the STAAR Math test can be a really daunting and boring task. What's the best way to go about it? Is there a certain study method that works better than others? Well, studying for the STAAR Math can be done effectively. The following six-step program has been designed to make preparing for the STAAR Grade 8 Math test more efficient and less overwhelming.

Step 1 - Create a study plan
Step 2 - Choose your study resources
Step 3 - Review, Learn, Practice
Step 4 - Learn and practice test-taking strategies
Step 5 - Learn the STAAR Grade 8 Test format and take practice tests
Step 6 - Analyze your performance

STEP 1: Create a Study Plan

It's always easier to get things done when you have a plan. Creating a study plan for the STAAR Grade 8 Math test can help you to stay on track with your studies. It's important to sit down and prepare a study plan with what works with your life, work, and any other obligations you may have. Devote enough time each day to studying. It's also a great idea to break down each section of the exam into blocks and study one concept at a time.

It's important to understand that there is no "right" way to create a study plan. Your study plan will be personalized based on your specific needs and learning style.

Follow these guidelines to create an effective study plan for your STAAR Grade 8 Math test:

★ **Analyze your learning style and study habits** – Everyone has a different learning style. It is essential to embrace your individuality and the unique way you learn. Think about what works and what doesn't work for you. Do you prefer STAAR Math prep books or a combination of textbooks and video lessons? Does it work better for you if you study every night for thirty minutes or is it more effective to study in the morning before going to work?

★ **Evaluate your schedule** – Review your current schedule and find out how much time you can consistently devote to STAAR Math study.

★ **Develop a schedule** – Now it's time to add your study schedule to your calendar like any other obligation. Schedule time for study, practice, and review. Plan out which topic you will study on which day to ensure that you're devoting enough time to each concept. Develop a study plan that is mindful, realistic, and flexible.

★ **Stick to your schedule** – A study plan is only effective when it is followed consistently. You should try to develop a study plan that you can follow for the length of your study program.

★ **Evaluate your study plan and adjust as needed** – Sometimes you need to adjust your plan when you have new commitments. Check in with yourself regularly to make sure that you're not falling behind in your study plan. Remember, the most important thing is sticking to your plan. Your study plan is all about helping you be more productive. If you find that your study plan is not as effective as you want, don't get discouraged. It's okay to make changes as you figure out what works best for you.

STEP 2: Choose Your Study Resources

There are numerous textbooks and online resources available for the STAAR Math test, and it may not be clear where to begin. Don't worry! This exercise book reviews all STAAR Grade 8 Math concepts and topics. In addition to the book content, you can also use Effortless Math's online resources. (video lessons, worksheets, formulas, etc.) On each page, there is a link (and a QR code) to an online webpage which provides a comprehensive review of the topic, step-by-step instruction, video tutorial, and numerous examples and exercises to help you fully understand the concept.

Simply visit <u>EffortlessMath.com/STAAR</u> to find your online STAAR Math resources.

STEP 3: Review, Learn, Practice

This STAAR Grade 8 Math exercise book breaks down each subject into specific skills or content areas. For instance, the percent concept is separated into different topics–percent calculation, percent increase and decrease, percent problems, etc. Use this book to help you go over all key math concepts and topics on the STAAR Grade 8 Math test.

As you review each topic, take notes or highlight the concepts you would like to go over again in the future. If you're unfamiliar with a topic or something is difficult for you, use the link (or the QR code) at the top of the page to find the webpage that provides more instruction about that topic. For each math topic, plenty of instructions, step-by-step guides, and examples are provided to ensure you get a good grasp of the material.

Quickly review the topics you do understand to get a brush-up of the material. Be sure to do the practice questions provided at the end of every chapter to measure your understanding of the concepts.

STEP 4: Learn and Practice Test-taking Strategies

In the following sections, you will find important test-taking strategies and tips that can help you earn extra points. You'll learn how to think strategically and when to guess if you don't know the answer to a question. Using STAAR Grade 8 Math test-taking strategies and tips can help you raise your score and do well on the test. Apply test taking strategies on the practice tests to help you boost your confidence.

STEP 5: Learn the STAAR Grade 8 Test Format and Take Practice Tests

The STAAR Grade 8 *Test Review* section provides information about the structure of the STAAR Grade 8 test. Read this section to learn more about the STAAR Grade 8 test structure, different test sections, the number of questions in each section, and the section time limits. When you have a prior understanding of the test format and different types of STAAR Grade 8 Math questions, you'll feel more confident when you take the actual exam.

Once you have read through the instructions and lessons and feel like you are ready to go – take advantage of both of the full-length STAAR Grade 8 Math practice tests available in this exercise book. Use the practice tests to sharpen your skills and build confidence.

The STAAR Grade 8 Math practice tests offered at the end of the book are formatted similarly to the actual STAAR Math test. When you take each practice test, try to simulate actual testing conditions. To take the practice tests, sit in a quiet space, time yourself, and work through as many of the questions as time allows. The practice tests are followed by detailed answer explanations to help you find your weak areas, learn from your mistakes, and raise your STAAR Math score.

STEP 6: Analyze Your Performance

After taking the practice tests, look over the answer keys and explanations to learn which questions you answered correctly and which you did not. Never be discouraged if you make a few mistakes. See them as a learning opportunity. This will highlight your strengths and weaknesses.

You can use the results to determine if you need additional practice or if you are ready to take the actual STAAR Math test.

Looking for more?

Visit EffortlessMath.com/STAAR to find hundreds of STAAR Grade 8 Math worksheets, video tutorials, practice tests, STAAR Grade 8 Math formulas, and much more.

Or scan this QR code.

No Registration Required.

STAAR Grade 8 Test Review

The State of Texas Assessments of Academic Readiness (STAAR) is developed under the supervision of the Texas Education Agency and is taken by all public-school students in Texas, grades 3–12. The tests measure the progress of students from 3rd grade to 8th grade, as well as high school. STAAR is the state's testing program and is based on state curriculum standards in core subjects including:

- Reading,
- Writing,
- Mathematics,
- Science,
- Social Studies

In high school, students take end-of-course STAAR exams in five high school subjects:

- Algebra I,
- Biology,
- English I,
- English II,
- U.S. History.

Students take STAAR tests in the spring. The number of tests a student takes each year will depend on what grade he or she is in. Most students will have two to four testing days during a school year.

In this book, there are Two complete Grade 8 STAAR Math Tests. Take these tests to see what score you'll be able to receive on a real STAAR Math test.

STAAR Math Test-Taking Strategies

Here are some test-taking strategies that you can use to maximize your performance and results on the STAAR Grade 8 Math test.

#1 : Use This Approach To Answer Every STAAR Math Question

1) Review the question to identify keywords and important information.
2) Translate the keywords into math operations so you can solve the problem.
3) Review the answer choices. What are the differences between answer choices?
4) Draw or label a diagram if needed.
5) Try to find patterns.
6) Find the right method to answer the question. Use straightforward math, plug in numbers, or test the answer choices (backsolving).
7) Double-check your work.

#2 : Use Educated Guessing

This approach is applicable to the problems you understand to some degree but cannot solve using straightforward math. In such cases, try to filter out as many answer choices as possible before picking an answer. In cases where you don't have a clue about what a certain problem entails, don't waste any time trying to eliminate answer choices. Just choose one randomly before moving onto the next question.

As you can ascertain, direct solutions are the most optimal approach. Carefully read through the question, determine what the solution is using the math you have learned before, then coordinate the answer with one of the choices available to you. Are you stumped? Make your best guess, then move on.

Don't leave any fields empty! Even if you're unable to work out a problem, strive to answer it. Take a guess if you have to. You will not lose points by getting an answer wrong, though you may gain a point by getting it correct!

#3 : BALLPARK

A ballpark answer is a rough approximation. When we become overwhelmed by calculations and figures, we end up making silly mistakes. A decimal that is moved by one unit can change an answer from right to wrong, regardless of the number of steps that you went through to get it. That's where ballparking can play a big part.

If you think you know what the correct answer may be (even if it's just a ballpark answer), you'll usually have the ability to eliminate a couple of choices. While answer choices are usually based on the average student error and/or values that are closely tied, you will still be able to weed out choices that are way far afield. Try to find answers that aren't in the proverbial ballpark when you're looking for a wrong answer on a multiple-choice question. This is an optimal approach to eliminating answers to a problem.

#4 : BACKSOLVING

A majority of questions on the STAAR Grade 8 Math test will be in multiple-choice format. Many test-takers prefer multiple-choice questions, as at least the answer is right there. You'll typically have four answers to pick from. You simply need to figure out which one is correct. Usually, the best way to go about doing so is "backsolving."

As mentioned earlier, direct solutions are the most optimal approach to answering a question. Carefully read through a problem, calculate a solution, then correspond the answer with one of the choices displayed in front of you. If you can't calculate a solution, your next best approach involves "backsolving."

When backsolving a problem, contrast one of your answer options against the problem you are asked, then see which of them is most relevant. More often than not, answer choices are listed in ascending or descending order. In such cases, try out the choices B or C. If it's not correct, you can go either down or up from there.

#5 : Plugging In Numbers

"Plugging in numbers" is a strategy that can be applied to a wide range of different math problems on the STAAR Grade 8 Math test. This approach is typically used to simplify a challenging question so that it is more understandable. By using the strategy carefully, you can find the answer without too much trouble.

The concept is fairly straightforward–replace unknown variables in a problem with certain values. When selecting a number, consider the following:

- Choose a number that's basic (just not too basic). Generally, you should avoid choosing 1 (or even 0). A decent choice is 2.

- Try not to choose a number that is displayed in the problem.

- Make sure you keep your numbers different if you need to choose at least two of them.

- More often than not, choosing numbers merely lets you filter out some of your answer choices. As such, don't just go with the first choice that gives you the right answer.

- If several answers seem correct, then you'll need to choose another value and try again. This time, though, you'll just need to check choices that haven't been eliminated yet.

- If your question contains fractions, then a potential right answer may involve either an LCD (least common denominator) or an LCD multiple.

- 100 is the number you should choose when you are dealing with problems involving percentages.

STAAR Grade 8 Math – Test Day Tips

After practicing and reviewing all the math concepts you've been taught, and taking some STAAR Grade 8 mathematics practice tests, you'll be prepared for test day. Consider the following tips to be extra-ready come test time.

Before Your Test

What to do the night before:

- **Relax!** One day before your test, study lightly or skip studying altogether. You shouldn't attempt to learn something new, either. There are plenty of reasons why studying the evening before a big test can work against you. Put it this way–a marathoner wouldn't go out for a sprint before the day of a big race. Mental marathoners–such as yourself–should not study for any more than one hour 24 hours before a STAAR Grade 8 test. That's because your brain requires some rest to be at its best. The night before your exam, spend some time with family or friends, or read a book.

- **Avoid bright screens** - You'll have to get some good shuteye the night before your test. Bright screens (such as the ones coming from your laptop, TV, or mobile device) should be avoided altogether. Staring at such a screen will keep your brain up, making it hard to drift asleep at a reasonable hour.

- **Make sure your dinner is healthy** - The meal that you have for dinner should be nutritious. Be sure to drink plenty of water as well. Load up on your complex carbohydrates, much like a marathon runner would do. Pasta, rice, and potatoes are ideal options here, as are vegetables and protein sources.

- **Get your bag ready for test day** - The night prior to your test, pack your bag with your stationery, ID, and any other gear that you need. Keep the bag right by your front door.

- **Make plans to reach the testing site** - Before going to sleep, ensure that you understand precisely how you will arrive at the site of the test. If parking is something you'll have to find first, plan for it. If you're dependent on public transit, then review the schedule. You should also make sure that the train/bus/subway/streetcar you use will be running. Find out about road closures as well. If a parent or friend is accompanying you, ensure that they understand what steps they have to take as well.

The Day of the Test

- Get up reasonably early, but not too early.

- Have breakfast - Breakfast improves your concentration, memory, and mood. As such, make sure the breakfast that you eat in the morning is healthy. The last thing you want to be is distracted by a grumbling tummy. If it's not your own stomach making those noises, another test taker close to you might be instead. Prevent discomfort or embarrassment by consuming a healthy breakfast. Bring a snack with you if you think you'll need it.

- Follow your daily routine - Do you exercise each morning while getting ready for the day? Don't break your usual habits on the day of the test. Likewise, if coffee isn't something you drink in the morning, then don't take up the habit hours before your test. Routine consistency lets you concentrate on the main objective–doing the best you can on your test.

- Wear layers - Dress yourself up in comfortable layers. You should be ready for any kind of internal temperature. If it gets too warm during the test, take a layer off.

- Get there on time - The last thing you want to do is get to the test site late. Rather, you should be there 45 minutes prior to the start of the test. Upon your arrival, try not to hang out with anybody who is nervous. Any anxious energy they exhibit shouldn't influence you.

- Leave the books at home - No books should be brought to the test site. If you start developing anxiety before the test, books could encourage you to do some last-minute studying, which will only hinder you. Keep the books far away–better yet, leave them at home.

- Make your voice heard - If something is off, speak to a proctor. If medical attention is needed or if you'll require anything, consult the proctor prior to the start of the test. Any doubts you have should be clarified. You should be entering the test site with a state of mind that is completely clear.

- **Have faith in yourself** - When you feel confident, you will be able to perform at your best. When you are waiting for the test to begin, envision yourself receiving an outstanding result. Try to see yourself as someone who knows all the answers, no matter what the questions are. A lot of athletes tend to use this technique–particularly before a big competition. Your expectations will be reflected by your performance.

During your test

- **Be calm and breathe deeply** - You need to relax before the test, and some deep breathing will go a long way to help you do that. Be confident and calm. You got this. Everybody feels a little stressed out just before an evaluation of any kind is set to begin. Learn some effective breathing exercises. Spend a minute meditating before the test starts. Filter out any negative thoughts you have. Exhibit confidence when having such thoughts.

- **Concentrate on the test** - Refrain from comparing yourself to anyone else. You shouldn't be distracted by the people near you or random noise. Concentrate exclusively on the test. If you find yourself irritated by surrounding noises, earplugs can be used to block sounds off close to you. Don't forget–the test is going to last several hours if you're taking more than one subject of the test. Some of that time will be dedicated to brief sections. Concentrate on the specific section you are working on during a particular moment. Do not let your mind wander off to upcoming or previous sections.

- **Skip challenging questions** - Optimize your time when taking the test. Lingering on a single question for too long will work against you. If you don't know what the answer is to a certain question, use your best guess, and mark the question so you can review it later on. There is no need to spend time attempting to solve something you aren't sure about. That time would be better served handling the questions you can actually answer well. You will not be penalized for getting the wrong answer on a test like this.

- **Try to answer each question individually** - Focus only on the question you are working on. Use one of the test-taking strategies to solve the problem. If you aren't able to come up with an answer, don't get frustrated. Simply skip that question, then move onto the next one.

- **Don't forget to breathe!** Whenever you notice your mind wandering, your stress levels boosting, or frustration brewing, take a thirty-second break. Shut your eyes, drop your pencil, breathe deeply, and let your shoulders relax. You will end up being more productive when you allow yourself to relax for a moment.

- **Review your answer.** If you still have time at the end of the test, don't waste it. Go back and check over your answers. It is worth going through the test from start to finish to ensure that you didn't make a sloppy mistake somewhere.

- **Optimize your breaks** - When break time comes, use the restroom, have a snack, and reactivate your energy for the subsequent section. Doing some stretches can help stimulate your blood flow.

After your test

- **Take it easy** - You will need to set some time aside to relax and decompress once the test has concluded. There is no need to stress yourself out about what you could've said, or what you may have done wrong. At this point, there's nothing you can do about it. Your energy and time would be better spent on something that will bring you happiness for the remainder of your day.

Contents

Contents

Contents

Chapter 1: Fractions and Mixed Numbers

Math Topics that you'll learn in this Chapter:

- ✓ Simplifying Fractions
- ✓ Adding and Subtracting Fractions
- ✓ Multiplying and Dividing Fractions
- ✓ Adding Mixed Numbers
- ✓ Subtracting Mixed Numbers
- ✓ Multiplying Mixed Numbers
- ✓ Dividing Mixed Numbers

Simplifying Fractions

✎ *Simplify each fraction.*

1) $\dfrac{8}{16} =$

2) $\dfrac{7}{21} =$

3) $\dfrac{11}{44} =$

4) $\dfrac{6}{24} =$

5) $\dfrac{6}{18} =$

6) $\dfrac{18}{27} =$

7) $\dfrac{15}{55} =$

8) $\dfrac{24}{54} =$

9) $\dfrac{63}{72} =$

10) $\dfrac{40}{64} =$

11) $\dfrac{23}{46} =$

12) $\dfrac{35}{63} =$

13) $\dfrac{32}{36} =$

14) $\dfrac{81}{99} =$

15) $\dfrac{16}{64} =$

16) $\dfrac{14}{35} =$

17) $\dfrac{19}{38} =$

18) $\dfrac{18}{54} =$

19) $\dfrac{56}{70} =$

20) $\dfrac{40}{45} =$

21) $\dfrac{9}{90} =$

22) $\dfrac{20}{25} =$

23) $\dfrac{36}{42} =$

24) $\dfrac{40}{48} =$

25) $\dfrac{18}{54} =$

26) $\dfrac{48}{144} =$

Adding and Subtracting Fractions

✎ *Calculate and write the answer in lowest term.*

6) $\frac{1}{3} + \frac{1}{5} =$

7) $\frac{2}{5} + \frac{3}{8} =$

8) $\frac{1}{3} - \frac{2}{9} =$

9) $\frac{4}{5} - \frac{2}{9} =$

10) $\frac{2}{9} + \frac{1}{3} =$

11) $\frac{3}{10} + \frac{2}{5} =$

12) $\frac{9}{10} - \frac{4}{5} =$

13) $\frac{7}{9} - \frac{3}{7} =$

14) $\frac{3}{4} + \frac{1}{3} =$

15) $\frac{3}{8} + \frac{2}{5} =$

16) $\frac{3}{4} - \frac{2}{5} =$

17) $\frac{7}{9} - \frac{2}{3} =$

18) $\frac{4}{9} + \frac{5}{6} =$

19) $\frac{2}{3} + \frac{1}{4} =$

20) $\frac{9}{10} - \frac{3}{5} =$

21) $\frac{7}{12} - \frac{1}{2} =$

22) $\frac{4}{5} + \frac{2}{3} =$

23) $\frac{5}{7} + \frac{1}{5} =$

24) $\frac{5}{9} - \frac{2}{5} =$

25) $\frac{3}{5} - \frac{2}{9} =$

26) $\frac{7}{9} + \frac{1}{7} =$

27) $\frac{5}{8} + \frac{2}{3} =$

28) $\frac{5}{7} - \frac{2}{5} =$

29) $\frac{7}{9} - \frac{3}{4} =$

30) $\frac{3}{5} - \frac{1}{6} =$

31) $\frac{3}{12} + \frac{2}{7} =$

Multiplying and Dividing Fractions

✏️ *Solve and write the answer in lowest term.*

1) $\frac{1}{3} \times \frac{9}{5} =$

2) $\frac{1}{4} \times \frac{3}{7} =$

3) $\frac{1}{5} \div \frac{1}{4} =$

4) $\frac{1}{6} \div \frac{5}{12} =$

5) $\frac{2}{3} \times \frac{4}{7} =$

6) $\frac{5}{7} \times \frac{3}{4} =$

7) $\frac{2}{5} \div \frac{3}{7} =$

8) $\frac{3}{7} \div \frac{5}{8} =$

9) $\frac{3}{8} \times \frac{4}{7} =$

10) $\frac{2}{9} \times \frac{6}{11} =$

11) $\frac{1}{10} \div \frac{3}{8} =$

12) $\frac{3}{10} \div \frac{4}{5} =$

13) $\frac{6}{7} \times \frac{4}{9} =$

14) $\frac{3}{7} \times \frac{5}{6} =$

15) $\frac{7}{9} \div \frac{6}{11} =$

16) $\frac{1}{15} \div \frac{2}{3} =$

17) $\frac{1}{13} \times \frac{1}{2} =$

18) $\frac{1}{12} \times \frac{4}{7} =$

19) $\frac{1}{15} \div \frac{4}{9} =$

20) $\frac{1}{16} \div \frac{1}{2} =$

21) $\frac{4}{7} \times \frac{5}{8} =$

22) $\frac{1}{11} \times \frac{4}{5} =$

23) $\frac{1}{16} \div \frac{5}{8} =$

24) $\frac{1}{15} \div \frac{2}{3} =$

25) $\frac{1}{13} \times \frac{2}{5} =$

26) $\frac{1}{18} \times \frac{3}{7} =$

Adding Mixed Numbers

✍ *Solve and write the answer in lowest terms.*

1) $1\frac{1}{5} + 2\frac{2}{5} =$

2) $1\frac{1}{2} + 4\frac{5}{6} =$

3) $2\frac{4}{5} + 2\frac{3}{10} =$

4) $3\frac{1}{6} + 2\frac{2}{5} =$

5) $1\frac{5}{6} + 1\frac{2}{5} =$

6) $3\frac{5}{7} + 1\frac{2}{9} =$

7) $3\frac{5}{8} + 2\frac{1}{3} =$

8) $1\frac{6}{7} + 3\frac{2}{9} =$

9) $2\frac{5}{9} + 1\frac{1}{4} =$

10) $3\frac{7}{9} + 2\frac{5}{6} =$

11) $2\frac{1}{10} + 2\frac{2}{5} =$

12) $1\frac{3}{10} + 3\frac{4}{5} =$

13) $3\frac{1}{12} + 2\frac{1}{3} =$

14) $5\frac{1}{11} + 1\frac{1}{2} =$

15) $3\frac{1}{21} + 2\frac{2}{3} =$

16) $4\frac{1}{24} + 1\frac{5}{8} =$

17) $2\frac{1}{25} + 3\frac{3}{5} =$

18) $3\frac{1}{15} + 2\frac{2}{10} =$

19) $5\frac{6}{7} + 2\frac{1}{3} =$

20) $2\frac{1}{8} + 3\frac{3}{4} =$

21) $2\frac{5}{7} + 2\frac{2}{21} =$

22) $4\frac{1}{6} + 1\frac{4}{5} =$

23) $2\frac{1}{7} + 2\frac{3}{8} =$

24) $3\frac{1}{4} + 2\frac{2}{3} =$

25) $1\frac{1}{13} + 2\frac{3}{4} =$

26) $3\frac{2}{35} + 2\frac{5}{7} =$

Subtracting Mixed Numbers

✎ *Solve and write the answer in lowest terms.*

1) $5\frac{2}{9} - 2\frac{1}{9} =$

2) $6\frac{2}{7} - 2\frac{1}{3} =$

3) $5\frac{3}{8} - 2\frac{3}{4} =$

4) $7\frac{2}{5} - 3\frac{1}{10} =$

5) $9\frac{5}{7} - 7\frac{4}{21} =$

6) $11\frac{7}{12} - 9\frac{5}{6} =$

7) $9\frac{5}{9} - 8\frac{1}{8} =$

8) $13\frac{7}{9} - 11\frac{3}{7} =$

9) $8\frac{7}{12} - 7\frac{3}{8} =$

10) $11\frac{5}{9} - 9\frac{1}{4} =$

11) $6\frac{5}{6} - 2\frac{2}{9} =$

12) $5\frac{7}{8} - 4\frac{1}{3} =$

13) $9\frac{5}{8} - 8\frac{1}{2} =$

14) $4\frac{9}{16} - 2\frac{1}{4} =$

15) $3\frac{2}{3} - 1\frac{2}{15} =$

16) $5\frac{1}{2} - 4\frac{2}{17} =$

17) $5\frac{6}{7} - 2\frac{1}{3} =$

18) $3\frac{3}{7} - 2\frac{2}{21} =$

19) $7\frac{3}{10} - 5\frac{2}{15} =$

20) $4\frac{5}{6} - 2\frac{2}{9} =$

21) $6\frac{3}{7} - 2\frac{2}{9} =$

22) $7\frac{4}{5} - 6\frac{3}{7} =$

23) $12\frac{3}{7} - 8\frac{1}{3} =$

24) $5\frac{4}{9} - 2\frac{5}{6} =$

25) $10\frac{1}{28} - 7\frac{3}{4} =$

26) $11\frac{5}{12} - 7\frac{5}{48} =$

Chapter 1: Fractions and Mixed Numbers

Multiplying Mixed Numbers

✒️ *Solve and write the answer in lowest terms.*

1) $1\frac{1}{6} \times 1\frac{3}{7} =$

2) $5\frac{1}{6} \times 2\frac{1}{4} =$

3) $3\frac{3}{7} \times 1\frac{2}{9} =$

4) $3\frac{3}{8} \times 3\frac{1}{6} =$

5) $1\frac{1}{2} \times 5\frac{2}{3} =$

6) $3\frac{1}{2} \times 6\frac{2}{3} =$

7) $9\frac{1}{2} \times 2\frac{1}{6} =$

8) $2\frac{5}{8} \times 8\frac{3}{5} =$

9) $3\frac{4}{5} \times 4\frac{2}{3} =$

10) $5\frac{1}{3} \times 2\frac{2}{7} =$

11) $6\frac{1}{3} \times 3\frac{3}{4} =$

12) $7\frac{2}{3} \times 1\frac{8}{9} =$

13) $8\frac{1}{2} \times 2\frac{1}{6} =$

14) $4\frac{1}{5} \times 8\frac{2}{3} =$

15) $3\frac{1}{8} \times 5\frac{2}{3} =$

16) $2\frac{2}{7} \times 6\frac{2}{5} =$

17) $2\frac{3}{8} \times 7\frac{2}{3} =$

18) $1\frac{7}{8} \times 8\frac{2}{3} =$

19) $9\frac{1}{2} \times 3\frac{1}{5} =$

20) $2\frac{5}{8} \times 4\frac{1}{3} =$

21) $6\frac{1}{3} \times 3\frac{2}{5} =$

22) $5\frac{3}{4} \times 2\frac{2}{7} =$

23) $8\frac{1}{6} \times 2\frac{2}{7} =$

24) $4\frac{1}{6} \times 7\frac{1}{5} =$

25) $2\frac{1}{5} \times 2\frac{5}{8} =$

26) $6\frac{2}{3} \times 4\frac{3}{5} =$

Dividing Mixed Numbers

✎ *Solve and write the answer in lowest terms.*

1) $6\frac{1}{2} \div 4\frac{2}{5} =$

2) $1\frac{3}{8} \div 1\frac{1}{4} =$

3) $6\frac{2}{5} \div 2\frac{4}{5} =$

4) $7\frac{1}{3} \div 6\frac{3}{4} =$

5) $7\frac{2}{5} \div 3\frac{3}{4} =$

6) $2\frac{4}{5} \div 3\frac{2}{3} =$

7) $8\frac{3}{5} \div 4\frac{3}{4} =$

8) $6\frac{3}{4} \div 2\frac{2}{9} =$

9) $5\frac{2}{7} \div 2\frac{2}{9} =$

10) $2\frac{2}{5} \div 3\frac{3}{5} =$

11) $4\frac{3}{7} \div 1\frac{7}{8} =$

12) $2\frac{5}{7} \div 2\frac{4}{5} =$

13) $8\frac{3}{5} \div 6\frac{1}{5} =$

14) $2\frac{5}{8} \div 1\frac{8}{9} =$

15) $5\frac{6}{7} \div 2\frac{3}{4} =$

16) $1\frac{3}{5} \div 2\frac{3}{8} =$

17) $5\frac{3}{4} \div 3\frac{2}{5} =$

18) $2\frac{3}{4} \div 3\frac{1}{5} =$

19) $3\frac{2}{3} \div 1\frac{2}{5} =$

20) $4\frac{1}{4} \div 2\frac{2}{3} =$

21) $3\frac{5}{6} \div 2\frac{4}{5} =$

22) $2\frac{1}{8} \div 1\frac{3}{4} =$

23) $5\frac{1}{2} \div 4\frac{2}{5} =$

24) $6\frac{3}{7} \div 2\frac{1}{7} =$

25) $3\frac{3}{6} \div 1\frac{5}{7} =$

26) $4\frac{4}{9} \div 4\frac{2}{3} =$

Answers – Chapter 1

Simplifying Fractions

1) $\frac{1}{2}$

2) $\frac{1}{3}$

3) $\frac{1}{4}$

4) $\frac{1}{4}$

5) $\frac{1}{3}$

6) $\frac{2}{3}$

7) $\frac{3}{11}$

8) $\frac{4}{9}$

9) $\frac{7}{8}$

10) $\frac{5}{8}$

11) $\frac{1}{2}$

12) $\frac{5}{9}$

13) $\frac{8}{9}$

14) $\frac{9}{11}$

15) $\frac{1}{4}$

16) $\frac{2}{5}$

17) $\frac{1}{2}$

18) $\frac{1}{3}$

19) $\frac{4}{5}$

20) $\frac{8}{9}$

21) $\frac{1}{10}$

22) $\frac{4}{5}$

23) $\frac{6}{7}$

24) $\frac{5}{6}$

25) $\frac{1}{3}$

26) $\frac{1}{3}$

Adding and Subtracting Fractions

1) $\frac{8}{15}$

2) $\frac{31}{40}$

3) $\frac{1}{9}$

4) $\frac{26}{45}$

5) $\frac{5}{9}$

6) $\frac{7}{10}$

7) $\frac{1}{10}$

8) $\frac{22}{63}$

9) $\frac{13}{12}$

10) $\frac{31}{40}$

11) $\frac{7}{20}$

12) $\frac{1}{9}$

13) $\frac{23}{18}$

14) $\frac{11}{12}$

15) $\frac{3}{10}$

16) $\frac{1}{12}$

17) $\frac{22}{15}$

18) $\frac{32}{35}$

19) $\frac{7}{45}$

20) $\frac{17}{45}$

21) $\frac{58}{63}$

22) $\frac{31}{24}$

23) $\frac{11}{35}$

24) $\frac{1}{36}$

25) $\frac{13}{30}$

26) $\frac{15}{28}$

Multiplying and Dividing Fractions

1) $\dfrac{3}{5}$

2) $\dfrac{3}{28}$

3) $\dfrac{4}{5}$

4) $\dfrac{2}{5}$

5) $\dfrac{8}{21}$

6) $\dfrac{15}{28}$

7) $\dfrac{14}{15}$

8) $\dfrac{24}{35}$

9) $\dfrac{3}{14}$

10) $\dfrac{4}{33}$

11) $\dfrac{4}{15}$

12) $\dfrac{3}{8}$

13) $\dfrac{8}{21}$

14) $\dfrac{5}{14}$

15) $\dfrac{77}{54}$

16) $\dfrac{1}{10}$

17) $\dfrac{1}{26}$

18) $\dfrac{1}{21}$

19) $\dfrac{3}{20}$

20) $\dfrac{1}{8}$

21) $\dfrac{5}{14}$

22) $\dfrac{4}{55}$

23) $\dfrac{1}{10}$

24) $\dfrac{1}{10}$

25) $\dfrac{2}{65}$

26) $\dfrac{1}{42}$

Adding Mixed Numbers

1) $3\dfrac{3}{5}$

2) $6\dfrac{1}{3}$

3) $5\dfrac{1}{10}$

4) $5\dfrac{17}{30}$

5) $3\dfrac{7}{30}$

6) $4\dfrac{59}{63}$

7) $5\dfrac{23}{24}$

8) $5\dfrac{5}{63}$

9) $3\dfrac{29}{36}$

10) $6\dfrac{11}{18}$

11) $4\dfrac{1}{2}$

12) $5\dfrac{1}{10}$

13) $5\dfrac{5}{12}$

14) $6\dfrac{13}{22}$

15) $5\dfrac{5}{7}$

16) $5\dfrac{2}{3}$

17) $5\dfrac{16}{25}$

18) $5\dfrac{4}{15}$

19) $8\dfrac{4}{21}$

20) $5\dfrac{7}{8}$

21) $4\dfrac{17}{21}$

22) $5\dfrac{29}{30}$

23) $4\dfrac{29}{56}$

24) $5\dfrac{11}{12}$

25) $3\dfrac{43}{52}$

26) $5\dfrac{27}{35}$

Subtracting Mixed Numbers

1) $3\frac{1}{9}$

2) $3\frac{20}{21}$

3) $2\frac{5}{8}$

4) $4\frac{3}{10}$

5) $2\frac{11}{21}$

6) $1\frac{3}{4}$

7) $1\frac{31}{72}$

8) $2\frac{22}{63}$

9) $1\frac{5}{24}$

10) $2\frac{11}{36}$

11) $4\frac{11}{18}$

12) $1\frac{13}{24}$

13) $1\frac{1}{8}$

14) $2\frac{5}{16}$

15) $2\frac{8}{15}$

16) $1\frac{13}{34}$

17) $3\frac{11}{21}$

18) $1\frac{1}{3}$

19) $2\frac{1}{6}$

20) $2\frac{11}{18}$

21) $4\frac{13}{63}$

22) $1\frac{13}{35}$

23) $4\frac{2}{21}$

24) $2\frac{11}{18}$

25) $2\frac{2}{7}$

26) $4\frac{5}{16}$

Multiplying Mixed Numbers

1) $1\frac{2}{3}$

2) $11\frac{5}{8}$

3) $4\frac{4}{21}$

4) $10\frac{11}{16}$

5) $8\frac{1}{2}$

6) $23\frac{1}{3}$

7) $20\frac{7}{12}$

8) $22\frac{23}{40}$

9) $17\frac{11}{15}$

10) $12\frac{4}{21}$

11) $23\frac{3}{4}$

12) $14\frac{13}{27}$

13) $18\frac{5}{12}$

14) $36\frac{2}{5}$

15) $17\frac{17}{24}$

16) $14\frac{22}{35}$

17) $18\frac{5}{24}$

18) $16\frac{1}{4}$

19) $30\frac{2}{5}$

20) $11\frac{3}{8}$

21) $21\frac{8}{15}$

22) $13\frac{1}{7}$

23) $18\frac{2}{3}$

24) 30

25) $5\frac{31}{40}$

26) $30\frac{2}{3}$

Dividing Mixed Numbers

1) $1\frac{21}{44}$

2) $1\frac{1}{10}$

3) $2\frac{2}{7}$

4) $1\frac{7}{81}$

5) $1\frac{73}{75}$

6) $\frac{42}{55}$

7) $1\frac{77}{95}$

8) $3\frac{3}{80}$

9) $2\frac{53}{140}$

10) $\frac{2}{3}$

11) $2\frac{88}{105}$

12) $\frac{95}{98}$

13) $1\frac{12}{31}$

14) $1\frac{53}{136}$

15) $2\frac{10}{77}$

16) $\frac{64}{95}$

17) $1\frac{47}{68}$

18) $\frac{55}{64}$

19) $2\frac{13}{21}$

20) $1\frac{19}{32}$

21) $1\frac{31}{84}$

22) $1\frac{3}{14}$

23) $1\frac{1}{4}$

24) 3

25) $2\frac{1}{24}$

26) $\frac{20}{21}$

Chapter 2: Decimal

Math Topics that you'll learn in this Chapter:

- ✓ Comparing Decimals
- ✓ Rounding Decimals
- ✓ Adding and Subtracting Decimals
- ✓ Multiplying and Dividing Decimals

13

Comparing Decimals

✎ *Compare. Use* >, =, *and* <

1) 0.44 ☐ 0.044

2) 0.67 ☐ 0.68

3) 0.49 ☐ 0.79

4) 1.35 ☐ 1.45

5) 1.58 ☐ 1.75

6) 2.91 ☐ 2.85

7) 14.56 ☐ 1.456

8) 17.85 ☐ 17.89

9) 21.52 ☐ 21.052

10) 11.12 ☐ 11.03

11) 9.650 ☐ 9.65

12) 8.578 ☐ 8.568

13) 3.15 ☐ 0.315

14) 16.61 ☐ 16.16

15) 18.581 ☐ 8.991

16) 25.05 ☐ 2.505

17) 4.55 ☐ 4.65

18) 0.158 ☐ 1.58

19) 0.881 ☐ 0.871

20) 0.505 ☐ 0.510

21) 0.772 ☐ 0.777

22) 0.5 ☐ 0.500

23) 16.89 ☐ 15.89

24) 12.25 ☐ 12.35

25) 5.82 ☐ 5.69

26) 1.320 ☐ 1.032

27) 0.082 ☐ 0.088

28) 0.99 ☐ 0.099

29) 2.360 ☐ 2.840

30) 0.330 ☐ 0.303

31) 16.44 ☐ 1.664

32) 0.424 ☐ 0.442

Rounding Decimals

✎ *Round each number to the underlined place value.*

1) 3.960 =

2) 4.372 =

3) 11.136 =

4) 17.5 =

5) 1.981 =

6) 14.215 =

7) 17.548 =

8) 25.508 =

9) 31.089 =

10) 69.345 =

11) 9.457 =

12) 12.901 =

13) 2.658 =

14) 32.565 =

15) 6.058 =

16) 98.108 =

17) 27.705 =

18) 36.75 =

19) 9.08 =

20) 7.185 =

21) 22.547 =

22) 66.098 =

23) 87.75 =

24) 18.541 =

25) 10.258 =

26) 13.456 =

27) 71.084 =

28) 29.23 =

29) 43.45 =

30) 81.07 =

31) 92.366 =

32) 24.76 =

Adding and Subtracting Decimals

✎ *Solve.*

1) $11.62 + 18.23 =$

2) $13.78 + 16.58 =$

3) $56.30 - 45.68 =$

4) $59.36 - 30.88 =$

5) $24.32 + 26.45 =$

6) $36.25 + 18.37 =$

7) $47.85 - 35.12 =$

8) $85.65 - 67.48 =$

9) $25.49 + 34.18 =$

10) $19.99 + 48.66 =$

11) $46.32 - 27.77 =$

12) $54.62 - 48.12 =$

13) $24.42 + 16.54 =$

14) $52.13 + 12.32 =$

15) $82.36 - 78.65 =$

16) $64.12 - 49.15 =$

17) $36.41 + 24.52 =$

18) $85.96 - 74.63 =$

19) $52.62 - 42.54 =$

20) $21.20 + 24.58 =$

21) $32.15 + 17.17 =$

22) $96.32 - 85.54 =$

23) $89.78 - 69.85 =$

24) $29.28 + 39.79 =$

25) $11.11 + 19.99 =$

26) $28.82 + 20.88 =$

27) $63.14 - 28.91 =$

28) $56.61 - 49.72 =$

29) $66.14 + 32.12 =$

30) $30.19 + 25.83 =$

31) $68.21 - 25.10 =$

32) $76.57 - 45.13 =$

Multiplying and Dividing Decimals

✎ **Solve.**

1) $12.3 \times 0.2 =$

2) $12.6 \times 0.9 =$

3) $54.4 \div 2 =$

4) $64.8 \div 8 =$

5) $23.1 \times 0.3 =$

6) $1.2 \times 0.7 =$

7) $5.5 \div 0.5 =$

8) $64.8 \div 8 =$

9) $1.4 \times 0.5 =$

10) $4.5 \times 0.3 =$

11) $88.8 \div 4 =$

12) $10.5 \div 5 =$

13) $2.2 \times 0.3 =$

14) $0.2 \times 0.52 =$

15) $95.7 \div 100 =$

16) $36.6 \div 6 =$

17) $3.2 \times 2 =$

18) $4.1 \times 0.5 =$

19) $68.4 \div 2 =$

20) $27.9 \div 9 =$

21) $3.5 \times 4 =$

22) $4.8 \times 0.5 =$

23) $6.4 \div 4 =$

24) $72.8 \div 0.8 =$

25) $1.8 \times 3 =$

26) $6.5 \times 0.2 =$

27) $93.6 \div 3 =$

28) $45.15 \div 0.5 =$

29) $12.6 \times 0.5 =$

30) $13.2 \times 6 =$

31) $6.4 \div 0.8 =$

32) $98.6 \div 0.2 =$

Answers – Chapter 2

Comparing Decimals

1) $0.44 > 0.044$

2) $0.67 < 0.68$

3) $0.49 < 0.79$

4) $1.35 < 1.45$

5) $1.58 < 1.75$

6) $2.91 > 2.85$

7) $14.56 > 1.456$

8) $17.85 < 17.89$

9) $21.52 > 21.052$

10) $11.12 > 11.03$

11) $9.650 = 9.65$

12) $8.578 > 8.568$

13) $3.15 > 0.315$

14) $16.61 > 16.16$

15) $18.581 > 8.991$

16) $25.05 > 2.505$

17) $4.55 < 4.65$

18) $0.158 < 1.58$

19) $0.881 > 0.871$

20) $0.505 < 0.510$

21) $0.772 < 0.777$

22) $0.5 = 0.500$

23) $16.89 > 15.89$

24) $12.25 < 12.35$

25) $5.82 > 5.69$

26) $1.320 > 1.032$

27) $0.082 < 0.088$

28) $0.99 > 0.099$

29) $2.360 < 2.840$

30) $0.330 > 0.303$

31) $16.44 > 1.664$

32) $0.424 < 0.442$

Rounding Decimals

1) $\underline{3}.960 = 4$

2) $4.3\underline{7}2 = 4.37$

3) $11.1\underline{3}6 = 11.14$

4) $1\underline{7}.5 = 18$

5) $1.9\underline{8}1 = 1.98$

6) $14.\underline{2}15 = 14.2$

7) $17.5\underline{4}8 = 17.55$

8) $25.5\underline{0}8 = 25.51$

9) $3\underline{1}.089 = 31$

10) $69.\underline{3}45 = 69.3$

11) $9.4\underline{5}7 = 9.46$

12) $1\underline{2}.901 = 13$

13) $2.6\underline{5}8 = 2.66$

14) $32.\underline{5}65 = 32.6$

15) $6.0\underline{5}8 = 6.06$

16) $98.1\underline{0}8 = 98.11$

17) $27.\underline{7}05 = 27.7$

18) $3\underline{6}.75 = 37$

19) $9.\underline{0}8 = 9.1$

20) $7.\underline{1}85 = 7.2$

21) $22.5\underline{4}7 = 22.55$

22) $66.\underline{0}98 = 66.1$

23) $8\underline{7}.75 = 88$

24) $18.\underline{5}41 = 18.5$

25) $10.2\underline{5}8 = 10.26$

26) $13.\underline{4}56 = 13.5$

27) $71.0\underline{8}4 = 71.08$

28) $2\underline{9}.23 = 29$

29) $43.\underline{4}5 = 43.5$

30) $8\underline{1}.07 = 81$

31) $9\underline{2}.366 = 92$

32) $24.\underline{7}6 = 24.8$

Adding and Subtracting Decimals

1) 29.85	9) 59.67	17) 60.93	25) 31.1
2) 30.36	10) 68.65	18) 11.33	26) 49.7
3) 10.62	11) 18.55	19) 10.08	27) 34.23
4) 28.48	12) 6.5	20) 45.78	28) 6.89
5) 50.77	13) 40.96	21) 49.32	29) 98.26
6) 54.62	14) 64.45	22) 10.78	30) 56.02
7) 12.73	15) 3.71	23) 19.93	31) 43.11
8) 18.17	16) 14.97	24) 69.07	32) 31.44

Multiplying and Dividing Decimals

1) 2.46	9) 0.7	17) 6.4	25) 5.4
2) 11.34	10) 1.35	18) 2.05	26) 1.3
3) 27.2	11) 22.2	19) 34.2	27) 31.2
4) 8.1	12) 2.1	20) 3.1	28) 90.3
5) 6.93	13) 0.66	21) 14	29) 6.3
6) 0.84	14) 0.104	22) 2.4	30) 79.2
7) 11	15) 0.957	23) 1.6	31) 8
8) 8.1	16) 6.1	24) 91	32) 493

Chapter 3: Integers and Order of Operations

Math Topics that you'll learn in this Chapter:

- ✓ Adding and Subtracting Integers
- ✓ Multiplying and Dividing Integers
- ✓ Order of Operations
- ✓ Integers and Absolute Value

21

Adding and Subtracting Integers

✏️ *Solve.*

1) $-(9) + 15 =$

2) $15 - (-11 - 9) =$

3) $(-10) + (-6) =$

4) $(-10) + (-6) + 7 =$

5) $-(23) + 19 =$

6) $(-7 + 5) - 9 =$

7) $28 + (-32) =$

8) $(-11) + (-9) + 5 =$

9) $25 - (8 - 7) =$

10) $-(29) + 17 =$

11) $(-38) + (-3) + 29 =$

12) $15 - (-7 + 9) =$

13) $24 - (8 - 2) =$

14) $(-7 + 4) - 9 =$

15) $(-17) + (-3) + 9 =$

16) $(-26) + (-7) + 8 =$

17) $(-9) + (-11) =$

18) $8 - (-23 - 13) =$

19) $(-16) + (-2) =$

20) $25 - (7 - 4) =$

21) $23 + (-12) =$

22) $(-18) + (-6) =$

23) $17 - (-21 - 7) =$

24) $-(28) - (-16) + 5 =$

25) $(-9 + 4) - 8 =$

26) $(-28) + (-6) + 17 =$

27) $-(21) - (-15) + 9 =$

28) $(-31) + (-6) =$

29) $(-18) + (-10) + 13 =$

30) $(-30) + (-11) + 12 =$

31) $-(28) - (-10) + 6 =$

32) $6 - (-16 - 11) =$

Multiplying and Dividing Integers

✎ *Solve.*

1) $(-6) \times (-7) =$

2) $8 \times (-5) =$

3) $48 \div (-8) =$

4) $(-72) \div 9 =$

5) $(4) \times (-6) =$

6) $(-9) \times (-11) =$

7) $(10) \div (-5) =$

8) $144 \div (-12) =$

9) $(10) \times (-2) =$

10) $(-8) \times (-2) \times 5 =$

11) $(8) \div (-2) =$

12) $45 \div (-15) =$

13) $(5) \times (-7) =$

14) $(-6) \times (-5) \times 4 =$

15) $(12) \div (-6) =$

16) $(14) \div (-7) =$

17) $196 \div (-14) =$

18) $(27 - 13) \times (-2) =$

19) $125 \div (-5) =$

20) $66 \div (-6) =$

21) $(-6) \times (-5) \times 3 =$

22) $(15 - 6) \times (-3) =$

23) $(32 - 24) \div (-4) =$

24) $72 \div (-6) =$

25) $(-14 + 8) \times (-7) =$

26) $(-3) \times (-9) \times 3 =$

27) $84 \div (-12) =$

28) $(-12) \times (-10) =$

29) $22 \times (-3) =$

30) $(-2) \times (-6) \times 5 =$

31) $(24) \div (-3) =$

32) $(-15) \div (3) =$

Order of Operation

✏ *Calculate.*

1) $16 + (30 \div 5) =$

2) $(3 \times 9) \div (-3) =$

3) $57 - (3 \times 8) =$

4) $(-12) \times (7 - 3) =$

5) $(18 - 7) \times (6) =$

6) $(6 \times 10) \div (12 + 3) =$

7) $(13 \times 2) - (24 \div 6) =$

8) $(-5) + (4 \times 3) + 8 =$

9) $(4 \times 2^3) + (16 - 9) =$

10) $(3^2 \times 7) \div (-2 + 1) =$

11) $[-2(48 \div 2^3)] - 6 =$

12) $(-4) + (7 \times 8) + 18 =$

13) $(3 \times 7) + (16 - 7) =$

14) $[3^3 \times (48 \div 2^3)] \div (-2) =$

15) $(14 \times 3) - (3^4 \div 9) =$

16) $(96 \div 12) \times (-3) =$

17) $(48 \div 2^2) \times (-2) =$

18) $(56 \div 7) \times (-5) =$

19) $(-2^2) + (7 \times 9) - 21 =$

20) $(2^4 - 9) \times (-6) =$

21) $[4^3 \times (50 \div 5^2)] \div (-16) =$

22) $(3^2 \times 4^2) \div (-4 + 2) =$

23) $6^2 - (-6 \times 4) + 3 =$

24) $4^2 - (5^2 \times 3) =$

25) $(-4) + (12^2 \div 3^2) - 7^2 =$

26) $(3^2 \times 5) + (-5^2 - 9) =$

27) $2[(3^2 \times 5) \times (-6)] =$

28) $(11^2 - 2^2) - (-7^2) =$

29) $(2^2 \times 5) - (64 \div 8) =$

30) $2[(3^2 \times 4) + (35 \div 5)] =$

31) $(4^2 \times 3) \div (-6) =$

32) $3^2[(4^3 \div 16) - (3^3 \div 27)] =$

Integers and Absolute Value

✎ *Calculate.*

1) $4 - |6 - 10| =$

2) $|14| - \dfrac{|-18|}{3} =$

3) $\dfrac{|8 \times -8|}{4} \times \dfrac{|-20|}{5} =$

4) $|12 \times 3| + \dfrac{|-81|}{9} =$

5) $4 - |11 - 18| - |3| =$

6) $|18| - \dfrac{|-12|}{4} =$

7) $\dfrac{|5 \times -8|}{10} \times \dfrac{|-22|}{11} =$

8) $|9 \times 3| + \dfrac{|-36|}{4} =$

9) $|-42 + 7| \times \dfrac{|-2 \times 5|}{10} =$

10) $6 - |17 - 11| - |5| =$

11) $|13| - \dfrac{|-54|}{6} =$

12) $\dfrac{|9 \times -4|}{12} \times \dfrac{|-45|}{9} =$

13) $|-75 + 50| \times \dfrac{|-4 \times 5|}{5} =$

14) $\dfrac{|-26|}{13} \times \dfrac{|-32|}{8} =$

15) $14 - |8 - 18| - |-12| =$

16) $|29| - \dfrac{|-20|}{5} =$

17) $\dfrac{|3 \times 8|}{2} \times \dfrac{|-33|}{3} =$

18) $|-45 + 15| \times \dfrac{|-12 \times 5|}{6} =$

19) $\dfrac{|-50|}{5} \times \dfrac{|-77|}{11} =$

20) $12 - |2 - 7| - |15| =$

21) $|18| - \dfrac{|-45|}{15} =$

22) $\dfrac{|7 \times 8|}{4} \times \dfrac{|-48|}{12} =$

23) $\dfrac{|30 \times 2|}{3} \times |-12| =$

24) $\dfrac{|-36|}{9} \times \dfrac{|-80|}{8} =$

25) $|-30 + 9| \times \dfrac{|-8 \times 5|}{8} =$

26) $|16| - \dfrac{|-18|}{3} =$

27) $12 - |10 - 24| + |5| =$

28) $|-38 + 8| \times \dfrac{|-5 \times 6|}{10} =$

Answers – Chapter 3

Adding and Subtracting Integers

1) 6	9) 24	17) −20	25) −13
2) 35	10) −12	18) 44	26) −17
3) −16	11) −12	19) −18	27) 3
4) −9	12) 13	20) 22	28) −37
5) −4	13) 18	21) 11	29) −15
6) −11	14) −12	22) −24	30) −29
7) −4	15) −11	23) 45	31) −12
8) −15	16) −25	24) −7	32) 33

Multiplying and Dividing Integers

1) 42	9) −20	17) −14	25) 42
2) −40	10) 80	18) −28	26) 81
3) −6	11) −4	19) −25	27) −7
4) −8	12) −3	20) −11	28) 120
5) −24	13) −35	21) 90	29) −66
6) 99	14) 120	22) −27	30) 60
7) −2	15) −2	23) −2	31) −8
8) −12	16) −2	24) −12	32) −5

Order of Operation

1) 22	9) 39	17) −24	25) −37
2) −9	10) −63	18) −40	26) 11
3) 33	11) −18	19) 38	27) −540
4) −48	12) 70	20) −42	28) 166
5) 66	13) 30	21) −8	29) 12
6) 4	14) −81	22) −72	30) 86
7) 22	15) 33	23) 63	31) −8
8) 15	16) −24	24) −59	32) 27

Integers and Absolute Value

1) 0	8) 36	15) −8	22) 56
2) 8	9) 35	16) 25	23) 240
3) 64	10) −5	17) 132	24) 40
4) 45	11) 4	18) 300	25) 105
5) −6	12) 15	19) 70	26) 10
6) 15	13) 100	20) −8	27) 3
7) 8	14) 8	21) 15	28) 90

Chapter 4: Ratios and Proportions

Math Topics that you'll learn in this Chapter:

- ✓ Simplifying Ratios
- ✓ Proportional Ratios
- ✓ Similarity and Ratios
- ✓ Simple Interest

Simplifying Ratios

✎ *Simplify each ratio.*

1) $3:21 =$ ___ : ___

2) $4:16 =$ ___ : ___

3) $\dfrac{2}{28} = -$

4) $\dfrac{18}{45} = -$

5) $10:30 =$ ___ : ___

6) $5:30 =$ ___ : ___

7) $\dfrac{34}{38} = -$

8) $\dfrac{45}{63} = -$

9) $10:45 =$ ___ : ___

10) $20:30 =$ ___ : ___

11) $\dfrac{40}{64} = -$

12) $\dfrac{10}{110} = -$

13) $8:12 =$ ___ : ___

14) $16:20 =$ ___ : ___

15) $\dfrac{24}{48} = -$

16) $\dfrac{21}{77} = -$

17) $8:24 =$ ___ : ___

18) 9 to $36 =$ ___ : ___

19) $\dfrac{64}{72} = -$

20) $\dfrac{45}{60} = -$

21) $12:15 =$ ___ : ___

22) $18:54 =$ ___ : ___

23) $\dfrac{36}{54} = -$

24) $\dfrac{48}{104} = -$

25) $12:48 =$ ___ : ___

26) $18:72 =$ ___ : ___

27) $\dfrac{15}{75} = -$

28) $\dfrac{46}{52} = -$

Proportional Ratios

✎ *Solve each proportion for x.*

1) $\frac{4}{7} = \frac{8}{x}$, $x =$ _____

2) $\frac{9}{12} = \frac{x}{8}$, $x =$ _____

3) $\frac{3}{5} = \frac{12}{x}$, $x =$ _____

4) $\frac{3}{10} = \frac{x}{50}$, $x =$ _____

5) $\frac{3}{11} = \frac{15}{x}$, $x =$ _____

6) $\frac{6}{15} = \frac{x}{45}$, $x =$ _____

7) $\frac{6}{19} = \frac{12}{x}$, $x =$ _____

8) $\frac{7}{16} = \frac{x}{32}$, $x =$ _____

9) $\frac{18}{21} = \frac{54}{x}$, $x =$ _____

10) $\frac{13}{15} = \frac{39}{x}$, $x =$ _____

11) $\frac{9}{13} = \frac{72}{x}$, $x =$ _____

12) $\frac{8}{30} = \frac{x}{180}$, $x =$ _____

13) $\frac{3}{19} = \frac{9}{x}$, $x =$ _____

14) $\frac{1}{3} = \frac{x}{90}$, $x =$ _____

15) $\frac{25}{45} = \frac{x}{9}$, $x =$ _____

16) $\frac{1}{6} = \frac{9}{x}$, $x =$ _____

17) $\frac{7}{9} = \frac{63}{x}$, $x =$ _____

18) $\frac{54}{72} = \frac{x}{8}$, $x =$ _____

19) $\frac{32}{40} = \frac{4}{x}$, $x =$ _____

20) $\frac{21}{42} = \frac{x}{6}$, $x =$ _____

21) $\frac{56}{72} = \frac{7}{x}$, $x =$ _____

22) $\frac{1}{14} = \frac{x}{42}$, $x =$ _____

23) $\frac{5}{7} = \frac{75}{x}$, $x =$ _____

24) $\frac{30}{48} = \frac{x}{8}$, $x =$ _____

25) $\frac{36}{88} = \frac{9}{x}$, $x =$ _____

26) $\frac{62}{68} = \frac{x}{34}$, $x =$ _____

27) $\frac{42}{60} = \frac{x}{10}$, $x =$ _____

28) $\frac{8}{9} = \frac{x}{108}$, $x =$ _____

29) $\frac{40}{6} = \frac{x}{3}$, $x =$ _____

30) $\frac{88}{121} = \frac{x}{11}$, $x =$ _____

31) $\frac{10}{24} = \frac{x}{48}$, $x =$ _____

32) $\frac{32}{80} = \frac{x}{10}$, $x =$ _____

Create Proportion

✍ *State if each pair of ratios form a proportion.*

1) $\frac{3}{8}$ and $\frac{24}{50}$

2) $\frac{3}{11}$ and $\frac{6}{22}$

3) $\frac{4}{5}$ and $\frac{16}{20}$

4) $\frac{5}{11}$ and $\frac{12}{33}$

5) $\frac{5}{10}$ and $\frac{15}{30}$

6) $\frac{4}{13}$ and $\frac{8}{24}$

7) $\frac{6}{9}$ and $\frac{24}{36}$

8) $\frac{7}{12}$ and $\frac{14}{20}$

9) $\frac{3}{8}$ and $\frac{27}{72}$

10) $\frac{12}{20}$ and $\frac{36}{60}$

11) $\frac{11}{12}$ and $\frac{55}{60}$

12) $\frac{12}{15}$ and $\frac{24}{25}$

13) $\frac{15}{19}$ and $\frac{20}{38}$

14) $\frac{10}{14}$ and $\frac{40}{56}$

15) $\frac{11}{13}$ and $\frac{44}{39}$

16) $\frac{15}{16}$ and $\frac{30}{32}$

17) $\frac{17}{19}$ and $\frac{34}{48}$

18) $\frac{5}{18}$ and $\frac{15}{54}$

19) $\frac{3}{14}$ and $\frac{18}{42}$

20) $\frac{7}{11}$ and $\frac{14}{32}$

21) $\frac{8}{11}$ and $\frac{32}{44}$

22) $\frac{8}{14}$ and $\frac{24}{54}$

✍ *Solve.*

23) The ratio of boys to girls in a class is $3:4$. If there are 27 boys in the class, how many girls are in that class? _____

24) The ratio of red marbles to blue marbles in a bag is $5:6$. If there are 66 marbles in the bag, how many of the marbles are red? _____

25) You can buy 6 cans of green beans at a supermarket for $3.60. How much does it cost to buy 48 cans of green beans? _____

Similarity and Ratios

✎ *Each pair of figures is similar. Find the missing side.*

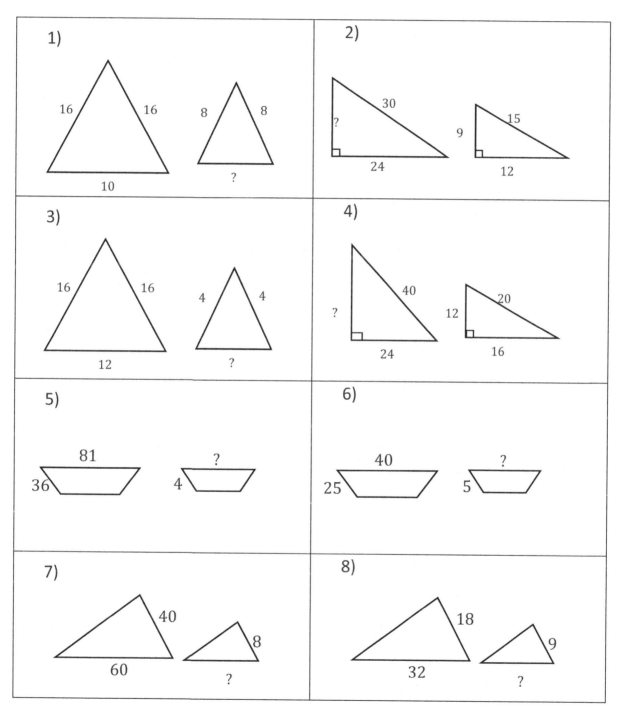

Chapter 4: Ratios and Proportions

Simple Interest

✍ *Determine the simple interest for these loans.*

1) $400 at 6% for 4 years. $___

2) $580 at 3.5% for 5 years. $_

3) $320 at 4% for 6 years. $___

4) $510 at 8% for 3 years. $___

5) $690 at 5% for 6 months. $___

6) $620 at 7% for 3 years. $___

7) $650 at 4.5% for 10 years. $___

8) $850 at 4% for 2 years. $___

9) $640 at 7% for 3 years. $___

10) $300 at 9% for 9 months. $___

11) $760 at 8% for 2 years. $_

12) $910 at 5% for 5 years. $___

13) $540 at 3% for 6 years. $___

14) $780 at 2.5% for 4 years. $___

15) $1,600 at 7% for 3 months. $___

16) $310 at 4% for 4 years. $___

17) $950 at 6% for 5 years. $___

18) $280 at 8% for 7 years. $___

19) $310 at 6% for 3 years. $___

20) $990 at 5% for 4 months. $___

21) $380 at 6% for 5 years. $___

22) $580 at 6% for 4 years. $___

23) $1,200 at 4% for 5 years. $___

24) $3,100 at 5% for 6 years. $___

25) $5,200 at 8% for 2 years. $___

26) $1,400 at 4% for 3 years. $___

27) $300 at 3% for 8 months. $___

28) $150 at 3.5% for 4 years. $___

29) $170 at 6% for 2 years. $___

30) $940 at 8% for 5 years. $___

31) $960 at 1.5% for 8 years. $_

32) $240 at 5% for 4 months. $___

33) $280 at 2% for 5 years. $___

34) $880 at 3% for 2 years. $___

35) $2,200 at 4.5% for 2 years. $___

36) $2,400 at 7% for 3 years. $___

37) $1,800 at 5% for 6 months. $___

38) $190 at 4% for 2 years. $___

39) $480 at 6% for 5 years. $___

40) $700 at 5% for 6 years. $_

Answers – Chapter 4

Simplifying Ratios

1) $1:7$

2) $1:4$

3) $\frac{1}{14}$

4) $\frac{2}{5}$

5) $1:3$

6) $1:6$

7) $\frac{17}{19}$

8) $\frac{5}{7}$

9) $2:9$

10) $2:3$

11) $\frac{5}{8}$

12) $\frac{1}{11}$

13) $2:3$

14) $4:5$

15) $\frac{1}{2}$

16) $\frac{3}{11}$

17) $1:3$

18) 1 to 4

19) $\frac{8}{9}$

20) $\frac{3}{4}$

21) $4:5$

22) $1:3$

23) $\frac{2}{3}$

24) $\frac{6}{13}$

25) $1:4$

26) $1:4$

27) $\frac{1}{5}$

28) $\frac{23}{26}$

Proportional Ratios

1) $x = 14$

2) $x = 6$

3) $x = 20$

4) $x = 15$

5) $x = 55$

6) $x = 18$

7) $x = 38$

8) $x = 14$

9) $x = 63$

10) $x = 45$

11) $x = 104$

12) $x = 48$

13) $x = 57$

14) $x = 30$

15) $x = 5$

16) $x = 54$

17) $x = 81$

18) $x = 6$

19) $x = 5$

20) $x = 3$

21) $x = 9$

22) $x = 3$

23) $x = 105$

24) $x = 5$

25) $x = 22$

26) $x = 31$

27) $x = 7$

28) $x = 96$

29) $x = 20$

30) $x = 8$

31) $x = 20$

32) $x = 4$

Create Proportion

1) *No*	10) *Yes*	19) *No*
2) *Yes*	11) *Yes*	20) *No*
3) *Yes*	12) *No*	21) *Yes*
4) *No*	13) *No*	22) *No*
5) *Yes*	14) *Yes*	23) 36 *girls*
6) *No*	15) *No*	24) 30 *red marbles*
7) *Yes*	16) *Yes*	25) $28.80
8) *No*	17) *No*	
9) *Yes*	18) *Yes*	

Similarity and Ratios

1) 5	5) 9
2) 18	6) 8
3) 3	7) 12
4) 32	8) 16

Simple Interest

1) $96

2) $101.50

3) $76.80

4) $122.40

5) $17.25

6) $130.20

7) $292.50

8) $68

9) $134.40

10) $20.25

11) $121.60

12) $227.50

13) $97.20

14) $78

15) $28

16) $49.60

17) $285

18) $156.80

19) $55.80

20) $16.5

21) $114

22) $139.20

23) $240

24) $930

25) $832

26) $168

27) $6

28) $21

29) $20.40

30) $376

31) $115.20

32) $4

33) $28

34) $52.80

35) $198

36) $504

37) $45

38) $15.20

39) $144

40) $210

Chapter 5:
Percentage

Math Topics that you'll learn in this Chapter:

- ✓ Percent Problems
- ✓ Percent of Increase and Decrease
- ✓ Discount, Tax and Tip

Percent Problems

✎ **Solve each problem.**

1) What is 4 percent of 280? ____

2) What is 25 percent of 500? ____

3) What is 10 percent of 460? ____

4) What is 34 percent of 260? ____

5) What is 60 percent of 850? ____

6) 63 is what percent of 300? ____%

7) 80 is what percent of 400? ____%

8) 70 is what percent of 700? ____%

9) 84 is what percent of 600? ___%

10) 90 is what percent of 300? ___%

11) 24 is what percent of 150? ___%

12) 12 is what percent of 80? ____%

13) 4 is what percent of 50? ____%

14) 110 is what percent of 500? _%

15) 16 is what percent of 400? _%

16) 39 is what percent of 300? ___%

17) 56 is what percent of 200? ___%

18) 30 is what percent of 500? ___%

19) 84 is what percent of 700? ___%

20) 40 is what percent of 500? __%

21) 26 is what percent of 100? __ %

22) 45 is what percent of 900? __%

23) 60 is what percent of 400? ___%

24) 18 is what percent of 900? ___%

25) 75 is what percent of 250? ___%

26) 27 is what percent of 900? ___%

27) 49 is what percent of 700? ___%

28) 81 is what percent of 900? ___%

29) 90 is what percent of 500? ___%

30) 82 is what percent of 410? ___%

31) 14 is 35 percent of what number? ____

32) 90 is 6 percent of what number? ____

33) 80 is 40 percent of what number? ____

34) 80 is 20 percent of what number? ____

35) 30 is 6 percent of what number? ____

36) 64 is 8 percent of what number? ____

Percent of Increase and Decrease

✎ *Solve each percent of change word problem.*

1) Bob got a raise, and his hourly wage increased from $30 to $42. What is the percent increase? _____ %

2) The price of gasoline rose from $4.40 to $4.62 in one month. By what percent did the gas price rise? _____ %

3) In a class, the number of students has been increased from 25 to 32. What is the percent increase? _____ %

4) The price of a pair of shoes increases from $24 to $30. What is the percent increase? ____ %

5) In a class, the number of students has been decreased from 24 to 18. What is the percentage decrease? _____ %

6) Nick got a raise, and his hourly wage increased from $50 to $55. What is the percent increase? _____ %

7) A coat was originally priced at $60. It went on sale for $54. What was the percent that the coat was discounted? _____ %

8) The price of a pair of shoes increases from $12 to $18. What is the percent increase? ____ %

9) A house was purchased in 2002 for $150,000. It is now valued at $132,000. What is the rate (percent) of depreciation for the house? _____ %

10) The price of gasoline rose from $4.00 to $4.20 in one month. By what percent did the gas price rise? _____ %

Discount, Tax and Tip

✍ *Find the missing values.*

1) Original price of a computer: $540, Tax: 6%, Selling price: $_____

2) Original price of a sofa: $400, Tax: 14%, Selling price: $_____

3) Original price of a table: $560, Tax: 15%, Selling price: $_____

4) Original price of a cell phone: $740, Tax: 24%, Selling price: $_____

5) Original price of a printer: $400, Tax: 22%, Selling price: $_____

6) Original price of a computer: $600, Tax: 15%, Selling price: $_____

7) Restaurant bill: $24.00, Tip: 25%, Final amount: $_____

8) Original price of a cell phone: $300 Tax: 8%, Selling price: $_____

9) Original price of a carpet: $800, Tax: 25%, Selling price: $_____

10) Original price of a camera: $200 Discount: 35%, Selling price: $_____

11) Original price of a dress: $560 Discount: 10%, Selling price: $___

12) Original price of a monitor: $420 Discount: 6%, Selling price: $____

13) Original price of a laptop: $880 Discount: 16%, Selling price: $____

14) Restaurant bill: $64.00, Tip: 20%, Final amount: $____

Answers – Chapter 5

Percent Problems

1) 11.2	13) 8%	25) 30%
2) 125	14) 22%	26) 3%
3) 46	15) 4%	27) 7%
4) 88.4	16) 13%	28) 9%
5) 510	17) 28%	29) 18%
6) 21%	18) 6%	30) 20%
7) 20%	19) 12%	31) 40
8) 10%	20) 8%	32) 1,500
9) 14%	21) 26%	33) 200
10) 30%	22) 5%	34) 400
11) 16%	23) 15%	35) 500
12) 15%	24) 2%	36) 800

Percent of Increase and Decrease

1) 40%	5) 25%	9) 12%
2) 5%	6) 10%	10) 5%
3) 28%	7) 10%	
4) 25%	8) 50%	

Discount, Tax and Tip

1) $572.40	6) $690	11) $504
2) $456	7) $30.00	12) $394.8
3) $644	8) $324	13) $739.2
4) $917.60	9) $1,000	14) $76.80
5) $488	10) $130	

Chapter 6:
Expressions and
Variables

Math Topics that you'll learn in this Chapter:

- ✓ Simplifying Variable Expressions
- ✓ Simplifying Polynomial Expressions
- ✓ Evaluating One Variable
- ✓ Evaluating Two Variables
- ✓ The Distributive Property

Simplifying Variable Expressions

✎ *Simplify and write the answer.*

1) $6x + 2 + 3x =$

2) $7x + 4 - 6x =$

3) $-1 - x^2 - 9x^2 =$

4) $(-5)(6x - 2) =$

5) $3 + 10x^2 + 2x =$

6) $8x^2 + 6x + 7x^2 =$

7) $2x^2 - 5x - 7x =$

8) $x - 3 + 5 - 3x =$

9) $2 - 3x + 12 - 2x =$

10) $5x^2 - 12x^2 + 8x =$

11) $2x^2 + 6x + 3x^2 =$

12) $2x^2 - 2x - x =$

13) $2x^2 - (-8x + 6) =$

14) $4x + 6(2 - 5x) =$

15) $10x + 8(10x - 6) =$

16) $9(-2x - 6) - 5 =$

17) $32x - 4 + 23 + 2x =$

18) $8x - 12x - x^2 + 13 =$

19) $(-6)(8x - 4) + 10x =$

20) $14x - 5(5 - 8x) =$

21) $23x + 4(9x + 3) + 12 =$

22) $3(-7x + 5) + 20x =$

23) $12x - 3x(x + 9) =$

24) $7x + 5x(3 - 3x) =$

25) $5x(-8x + 12) + 14x =$

26) $40x + 12 + 2x^2 =$

27) $5x(x - 3) - 10 =$

28) $8x - 7 + 8x + 2x^2 =$

29) $6x - 2x^2 - 6x^2 - 5 =$

30) $3 + x^2 - 4x^2 - 10x =$

31) $10x + 6x^2 + 5x + 18 =$

32) $20 + 12x^2 + 7x - 6x^2 =$

Simplifying Polynomial Expressions

✎ *Simplify and write the answer.*

1) $(3x^3 + 4x^2) - (10x + 3x^2) = $ _____

2) $(-4x^5 + 4x^3) - (6x^3 + 5x^2) = $ _____

3) $(10x^4 + 6x^2) - (x^2 - 8x^4) = $ _____

4) $6x - 2x^2 - 3(2x^2 + 5x^3) = $ _____

5) $(2x^3 - 3) + 3(2x^2 - 3x^3) = $ _____

6) $4(4x^3 - 2x) - (3x^3 - 2x^4) = $ _____

7) $2(4x - 3x^3) - 3(3x^3 + 4x^2) = $ _____

8) $(2x^2 - 2x) - (2x^3 + 5x^2) = $ _____

9) $2x^3 - (4x^4 + 2x) + x^2 = $ _____

10) $x^4 - 9(x^2 + x) - 5x = $ _____

11) $(-2x^2 - x^4) + (4x^4 - x^2) = $ _____

12) $4x^2 - 5x^3 + 15x^4 - 12x^3 = $ _____

13) $3x^2 - 2x^4 + 12x^4 - 10x^3 = $ _____

14) $4x^2 + 6x^3 - 8x^2 + 14x = $ _____

15) $3x^4 - 6x^5 + 7x^4 - 9x^2 = $ _____

16) $5x^3 + 15x - 4x^2 - 3x^3 = $ _____

Evaluating One Variable

✍ *Evaluate each expression using the value given.*

1) $x = 2 \Rightarrow 5x - 10 =$

2) $x = 3 \Rightarrow 6x - 12 =$

3) $x = 4 \Rightarrow 6x + 8 =$

4) $x = 6 \Rightarrow 2x + 4 =$

5) $x = 4 \Rightarrow 4x - 8 =$

6) $x = 2 \Rightarrow 5x - 2x + 10 =$

7) $x = 3 \Rightarrow 2x - x - 6 =$

8) $x = 4 \Rightarrow 6x - 3x + 4 =$

9) $x = -2 \Rightarrow 4x - 6x - 5 =$

10) $x = -1 \Rightarrow 3x - 5x + 11 =$

11) $x = 1 \Rightarrow x - 7x + 12 =$

12) $x = 2 \Rightarrow 2(-3x + 4) =$

13) $x = 3 \Rightarrow 4(-5x - 2) =$

14) $x = 2 \Rightarrow 5(-2x - 4) =$

15) $x = -2 \Rightarrow 3(-4x - 5) =$

16) $x = 3 \Rightarrow 8x + 5 =$

17) $x = -3 \Rightarrow 12x + 9 =$

18) $x = -1 \Rightarrow 9x - 8 =$

19) $x = 2 \Rightarrow 16x - 10 =$

20) $x = 1 \Rightarrow 4x + 3 =$

21) $x = 5 \Rightarrow 7x - 2 =$

22) $x = 7 \Rightarrow 28 - x =$

23) $x = 8 \Rightarrow 4x - 12 =$

24) $x = 10 \Rightarrow 44 - 3x =$

25) $x = 4 \Rightarrow 10x - 6 =$

26) $x = 7 \Rightarrow 6x - x + 9 =$

Evaluating Two Variables

✎ *Evaluate each expression using the values given.*

1) $x + 4y, x = 3, y = 2$ _____

2) $6x + 3y, x = -2, y = -3$ _____

3) $x + 5y, x = 2, y = -1$ _____

4) $3a - (10 - b), a = 3, b = 4$ _____

5) $4a - (6 - 3b), a = 1, b = 4$ _____

6) $a - (8 - 2b), a = 2, b = 5$ _____

7) $3z + 21 + 5k, z = 4, k = 1$ _____

8) $-7a + 4b, a = 6, b = 3$ _____

9) $-4a + 3b, a = 2, b = 4$ _____

10) $-6a + 6b, a = 4, b = 3$ _____

11) $-8a + 2b, a = 4, b = 6$ _____

12) $4x + 6y, x = 6, y = 3$ _____

13) $2x + 9y, x = 8, y = 1$ _____

14) $x - 7y, x = 9, y = 4$ _____

15) $5x - 4y, x = 6, y = 3$ _____

16) $2z + 14 + 8k, z = 4, k = 1$ _____

17) $6x + 3y, x = 3, y = 8$ _____

18) $5a - 6b, a = -3, b = -1$ _____

19) $6a + 2b, a = -6, b = 4$ _____

20) $-3a - b, a = 5, b = -6$ _____

21) $-6a + 2b, a = 6, b = -3$ _____

22) $-6a + 8b, a = 6, b = -1$ _____

The Distributive Property

✍ *Use the distributive property to simply each expression.*

1) $(-2)(10x + 3) =$

2) $(-3x + 5)(-5) =$

3) $11(-3x + 3) =$

4) $6(5 - 4x) =$

5) $(6 - 5x)(-4) =$

6) $9(8 - 2x) =$

7) $(-4x + 6)5 =$

8) $(-2x + 7)(-8) =$

9) $8(-4x + 7) =$

10) $(-9x + 5)(-3) =$

11) $8(-x + 9) =$

12) $7(2 - 6x) =$

13) $(-12x + 4)(-3) =$

14) $(-6)(-10x + 6) =$

15) $(-5)(5 - 11x) =$

16) $9(4 - 8x) =$

17) $(-6x + 2)7 =$

18) $(-9)(1 - 12x) =$

19) $(-3)(4 - 6x) =$

20) $(2 - 8x)(-2) =$

21) $20(2 - x) =$

22) $12(-4x + 3) =$

23) $12(3 - 4x) =$

24) $(-6x + 6)3 =$

25) $(-10x + 6)(-3) =$

26) $13(4 - 7x) =$

Answers – Chapter 6

Simplifying Variable Expressions

1) $9x + 2$

2) $x + 4$

3) $-10x^2 - 1$

4) $-30x + 10$

5) $10x^2 + 2x + 3$

6) $15x^2 + 6x$

7) $2x^2 - 12x$

8) $-2x + 2$

9) $-5x + 14$

10) $-7x^2 + 8x$

11) $5x^2 + 6x$

12) $2x^2 - 3x$

13) $2x^2 + 8x - 6$

14) $-26x + 12$

15) $90x - 48$

16) $-18x - 59$

17) $34x + 19$

18) $-x^2 - 4x + 13$

19) $-38x + 24$

20) $54x - 25$

21) $59x + 24$

22) $-x + 15$

23) $-3x^2 - 15x$

24) $-15x^2 + 22x$

25) $-40x^2 + 74x$

26) $2x^2 + 40x + 12$

27) $5x^2 - 15x - 10$

28) $2x^2 + 16x - 7$

29) $-8x^2 + 6x - 5$

30) $-3x^2 - 10x + 3$

31) $6x^2 + 15x + 18$

32) $6x^2 + 7x + 20$

Simplifying Polynomial Expressions

1) $3x^3 + x^2 - 10x$

2) $-4x^5 - 2x^3 - 5x^2$

3) $18x^4 + 5x^2$

4) $-15x^3 - 8x^2 + 6x$

5) $-7x^3 + 6x^2 - 3$

6) $2x^4 + 13x^3 - 8x$

7) $-15x^3 - 12x^2 + 8x$

8) $-2x^3 - 3x^2 - 2x$

9) $-4x^4 + 2x^3 + x^2 - 2x$

10) $x^4 - 9x^2 - 14x$

11) $3x^4 - 3x^2$

12) $15x^4 - 17x^3 + 4x^2$

13) $10x^4 - 10x^3 + 3x^2$

14) $6x^3 - 4x^2 + 14x$

15) $-6x^5 + 10x^4 - 9x^2$

16) $2x^3 - 4x^2 + 15x$

Evaluating One Variable

1) 0

2) 6

3) 32

4) 16

5) 8

6) 16

7) −3

8) 16

9) −1

10) 13

11) 6

12) −4

13) −68

14) −40

15) 9

16) 29

17) −27

18) −17

19) 22

20) 7

21) 33

22) 21

23) 20

24) 14

25) 34

26) 44

Evaluating Two Variables

1) 11

2) −21

3) −3

4) 3

5) 10

6) 4

7) 38

8) −30

9) 4

10) −6

11) −20

12) 42

13) 25

14) −19

15) 18

16) 30

17) 42

18) −9

19) −28

20) −9

21) −42

22) −44

The Distributive Property

1) $-20x - 6$

2) $15x - 25$

3) $-33x + 33$

4) $-24x + 30$

5) $20x - 24$

6) $-18x + 72$

7) $-20x + 30$

8) $16x - 56$

9) $-32x + 56$

10) $27x - 15$

11) $-8x + 72$

12) $-42x + 14$

13) $36x - 12$

14) $60x - 36$

15) $55x - 25$

16) $-72x + 36$

17) $-42x + 14$

18) $108x - 9$

19) $18x - 12$

20) $16x - 4$

21) $-20x + 40$

22) $-48x + 36$

23) $-48x + 36$

24) $-18x + 18$

25) $30x - 18$

26) $-91x + 52$

Chapter 7: Equations and Inequalities

Math Topics that you'll learn in this Chapter:

- ✓ One–Step Equations
- ✓ Multi–Step Equations
- ✓ System of Equations
- ✓ Graphing Single–Variable Inequalities
- ✓ One–Step Inequalities
- ✓ Multi–Step Inequalities

Chapter 7: Equations and Inequalities

One-Step Equations

✒ *Solve each equation for x.*

1) $x - 18 = 28 \Rightarrow x =$ _____

2) $19 = -5 + x \Rightarrow x =$ _____

3) $15 - x = 6 \Rightarrow x =$ _____

4) $x - 24 = 29 \Rightarrow x =$ _____

5) $24 - x = 17 \Rightarrow x =$ _____

6) $16 - x = 3 \Rightarrow x =$ _____

7) $x + 14 = 12 \Rightarrow x =$ _____

8) $26 + x = 8 \Rightarrow x =$ _____

9) $x + 9 = -18 \Rightarrow x =$ _____

10) $x + 21 = 11 \Rightarrow x =$ _____

11) $17 = -5 + x \Rightarrow x =$ _____

12) $x + 20 = 29 \Rightarrow x =$ _____

13) $x - 13 = 19 \Rightarrow x =$ _____

14) $x + 9 = -17 \Rightarrow x =$ _____

15) $x + 4 = -23 \Rightarrow x =$ _____

16) $16 = -9 + x \Rightarrow x =$ _____

17) $4x = 28 \Rightarrow x =$ _____

18) $21 = -7x \Rightarrow x =$ _____

19) $12x = -12 \Rightarrow x =$ _____

20) $13x = 39 \Rightarrow x =$ _____

21) $8x = -16 \Rightarrow x =$ _____

22) $\frac{x}{2} = -5 \Rightarrow x =$ _____

23) $\frac{x}{9} = 6 \Rightarrow x =$ _____

24) $27 = \frac{x}{5} \Rightarrow x =$ _____

25) $\frac{x}{4} = -3 \Rightarrow x =$ _____

26) $x \div 8 = 7 \Rightarrow x =$ _____

27) $x \div 2 = -3 \Rightarrow x =$ _____

28) $8x = 56 \Rightarrow x =$ _____

29) $9x = 54 \Rightarrow x =$ _____

30) $7x = -35 \Rightarrow x =$ _____

31) $60 = -10x \Rightarrow x =$ _____

Multi –Step Equations

✒ *Solve each equation.*

1) $4x - 7 = 13 \Rightarrow x =$ ____

2) $26 = -(x - 4) \Rightarrow x =$ ____

3) $-(5 - x) = 19 \Rightarrow x =$ ____

4) $35 = -x + 14 \Rightarrow x =$ ____

5) $2(3 - 2x) = 10 \Rightarrow x =$ ____

6) $3x - 3 = 15 \Rightarrow x =$ ____

7) $32 = -x + 15 \Rightarrow x =$ ____

8) $-(10 - x) = -13 \Rightarrow x =$ ____

9) $-4(7 + x) = 4 \Rightarrow x =$ ____

10) $22 = 2x - 8 \Rightarrow x =$ ____

11) $-6(3 + x) = 6 \Rightarrow x =$ ____

12) $-3 = 3x - 15 \Rightarrow x =$ ____

13) $-7(12 + x) = 7 \Rightarrow x =$ ____

14) $8(6 - 4x) = 16 \Rightarrow x =$ ____

15) $18 - 4x = -9 - x \Rightarrow x =$ ____

16) $6(4 - x) = 30 \Rightarrow x =$ ____

17) $15 - 3x = -5 - x \Rightarrow x =$ ____

18) $9(-7 - 3x) = 18 \Rightarrow x =$ ____

19) $16 - 2x = -4 - 7x \Rightarrow x =$ ____

20) $14 - 2x = 14 + x \Rightarrow x =$ ____

21) $21 - 3x = -7 - 10x \Rightarrow x =$ __

22) $8 - 2x = 11 + x \Rightarrow x =$ ____

23) $10 + 12x = -8 + 6x \Rightarrow x =$ __

24) $25 + 20x = -5 + 5x \Rightarrow x =$ __

25) $16 - x = -8 - 7x \Rightarrow x =$ ____

26) $17 - 3x = 13 + x \Rightarrow x =$ ____

27) $22 + 5x = -8 - x \Rightarrow x =$ ____

28) $-9(7 + x) = 9 \Rightarrow x =$ ____

29) $12 + 2x = -4 - 2x \Rightarrow x =$ ____

30) $12 - x = 2 - 3x \Rightarrow x =$ ____

31) $19 - x = -1 - 11x \Rightarrow x =$ ____

32) $14 - 3x = -5 - 4x \Rightarrow x =$ ____

System of Equations

✎ *Solve each system of equations.*

1) $2x + 3y = 15$ $x =$
    $x - 3y = 3$ $y =$

2) $y = x + 3$ $x =$
    $x + y = -5$ $y =$

3) $x + 3y = 6$ $x =$
    $2x + 8y = -12$ $y =$

4) $2x + y = 5$ $x =$
    $-3x + 6y = 0$ $y =$

5) $10x - 8y = -15$ $x =$
    $-6x + 4y = 13$ $y =$

6) $-3x - 4y = 5$ $x =$
    $x - 2y = 5$ $y =$

7) $5x - 12y = -19$ $x =$
    $-6x + 7y = 8$ $y =$

8) $5x - 7y = -2$ $x =$
    $-x - 2y = -3$ $y =$

9) $-x + 3y = 3$ $x =$
    $-7x + 8y = -5$ $y =$

10) $-4x + 3y = -18$ $x =$
    $4x - y = 14$ $y =$

11) $6x - 7y = -8$ $x =$
    $-x - 4y = -9$ $y =$

12) $-3x + 2y = -16$ $x =$
    $4x - y = 13$ $y =$

13) $2x + 3y = 8$ $x =$
    $-3x + 2y = 1$ $y =$

14) $y = -x + 3$ $x =$
    $3y + 5x = -1$ $y =$

15) $2x + 3y = 12$ $x =$
    $x + y = 5$ $y =$

16) $y = x - 1$ $x =$
    $y = 2x + 2$ $y =$

Graphing Single–Variable Inequalities

✎ *Graph each inequality.*

1) $x < 5$

2) $x \geq 2$

3) $x \geq -4$

4) $x \leq -1$

5) $x > -1$

6) $3 > x$

7) $2 \leq x$

8) $x > 0$

9) $-3 \leq x$

10) $-4 \leq x$

11) $x \leq 6$

12) $1 \leq x$

13) $-4 < x$

14) $x > -5$

One–Step Inequalities

✍ *Solve each inequality for* x.

1) $x - 9 < 20 \Rightarrow$ _____

2) $14 \leq -6 + x \Rightarrow$ _____

3) $x - 31 > 9 \Rightarrow$ _____

4) $x + 28 \geq 36 \Rightarrow$ _____

5) $x - 24 > 17 \Rightarrow$ _____

6) $x + 5 \geq 3 \Rightarrow x$_____

7) $x + 14 < 12 \Rightarrow$ _____

8) $26 + x \leq 8 \Rightarrow$ _____

9) $x + 9 \geq -18 \Rightarrow$ _____

10) $x + 24 < 11 \Rightarrow$ _____

11) $17 \leq -5 + x \Rightarrow$ _____

12) $x + 25 > 29 \Rightarrow x$_____

13) $x - 17 \geq 19 \Rightarrow$ _____

14) $x + 8 > -17 \Rightarrow$ _____

15) $x + 8 < -23 \Rightarrow$ _____

16) $16 \leq -5 + x \Rightarrow$ _____

17) $4x \leq 12 \Rightarrow$ _____

18) $28 \geq -7x \Rightarrow$ _____

19) $2x > -14 \Rightarrow$ _____

20) $13x \leq 39 \Rightarrow$ _____

21) $-8x > -16 \Rightarrow$ _____

22) $\frac{x}{2} < -6 \Rightarrow$ _____

23) $\frac{x}{6} > 6 \Rightarrow$ _____

24) $27 \leq \frac{x}{4} \Rightarrow$ _____

25) $\frac{x}{8} < -3 \Rightarrow$ _____

26) $6x \geq 18 \Rightarrow$ _____

27) $5x \geq -25 \Rightarrow$ _____

28) $3x > 45 \Rightarrow$ _____

29) $9x \leq 72 \Rightarrow$ _____

30) $-6x < -36 \Rightarrow$ _____

31) $70 > -10x \Rightarrow$ _____

Multi –Step Inequalities

✎ *Solve each inequality.*

1) $2x - 6 \leq 4 \rightarrow$ _____

2) $2 + 3x \geq 17 \rightarrow$ _____

3) $9 + 3x \geq 36 \rightarrow$ _____

4) $2x - 6 \leq 18 \rightarrow$ _____

5) $3x - 4 \leq 23 \rightarrow$ _____

6) $7x - 5 \leq 51 \rightarrow$ _____

7) $4x - 9 \leq 27 \rightarrow$ _____

8) $6x - 11 \leq 13 \rightarrow$ _____

9) $5x - 7 \leq 33 \rightarrow$ _____

10) $6 + 2x \geq 28 \rightarrow$ _____

11) $8 + 3x \geq 35 \rightarrow$ _____

12) $4 + 6x < 34 \rightarrow$ _____

13) $3 + 2x \geq 53 \rightarrow$ _____

14) $7 - 6x > 56 + x \rightarrow$ _____

15) $9 + 4x \geq 39 + 2x \rightarrow$ _____

16) $3 + 5x \geq 43 \rightarrow$ _____

17) $4 - 7x < 60 \rightarrow$ _____

18) $11 - 4x \geq 55 \rightarrow$ _____

19) $12 + x \geq 48 - 2x \rightarrow$ _____

20) $10 - 10x \leq -20 \rightarrow$ _____

21) $5 - 9x \geq -40 \rightarrow$ _____

22) $8 - 7x \geq 36 \rightarrow$ _____

23) $6 + 10x < 69 + 3x \rightarrow$ _____

24) $5 + 4x < 26 - 3x \rightarrow$ _____

25) $10 + 11x < 59 + 4x \rightarrow$ _____

26) $3 + 9x \geq 48 - 6x \rightarrow$ _____

Answers – Chapter 7

One–Step Equations

1) $x = 46$

2) $x = 24$

3) $x = 9$

4) $x = 53$

5) $x = 7$

6) $x = 13$

7) $x = -2$

8) $x = -18$

9) $x = -27$

10) $x = -10$

11) $x = 22$

12) $x = 9$

13) $x = 32$

14) $x = -26$

15) $x = -27$

16) $x = 25$

17) $x = 7$

18) $x = -3$

19) $x = -1$

20) $x = 3$

21) $x = -2$

22) $x = -10$

23) $x = 54$

24) $x = 135$

25) $x = -12$

26) $x = 56$

27) $x = -6$

28) $x = 7$

29) $x = 6$

30) $x = -5$

31) $x = -6$

Multi –Step Equations

1) $x = 5$

2) $x = -22$

3) $x = 24$

4) $x = -21$

5) $x = -1$

6) $x = 6$

7) $x = -17$

8) $x = -3$

9) $x = -8$

10) $x = 15$

11) $x = -4$

12) $x = 4$

13) $x = -13$

14) $x = 1$

15) $x = 9$

16) $x = -1$

17) $x = 10$

18) $x = -3$

19) $x = -4$

20) $x = 0$

21) $x = -4$

22) $x = -1$

23) $x = -3$

24) $x = -2$

25) $x = -4$

26) $x = 1$

27) $x = -5$

28) $x = -8$

29) $x = -4$

30) $x = -5$

31) $x = -2$

32) $x = -19$

System of Equations

1) $x = 6, y = 1$

2) $x = -4, y = -1$

3) $x = 42, y = -12$

4) $x = 2, y = 1$

5) $x = -\frac{11}{2}, y = -5$

6) $x = 1, y = -2$

7) $x = 1, y = 2$

8) $x = 1, y = 1$

9) $x = 3, y = 2$

10) $x = 3, y = -2$

11) $x = 1, y = 2$

12) $x = 2, y = -5$

13) $x = 1, y = 2$

14) $x = -5, y = 8$

15) $x = 3, y = 2$

16) $x = -3, y = -4$

Graphing Single–Variable Inequalities

1) $x < 5$

2) $x \geq 2$

3) $x \geq -4$

4) $x \leq -1$

5) $x > -1$

6) $3 > x$

7) $2 \leq x$

8) $x > 0$

9) $-3 \leq x$

10) $-4 \leq x$

11) $x \leq 6$

12) $1 \leq x$

13) $-4 < x$

14) $x > -5$

One–Step Inequalities

1) $x < 29$

2) $20 \leq x$

3) $x > 40$

4) $x \geq 8$

5) $x > 41$

6) $x \geq -2$

7) $x < -2$

8) $x \leq -18$

9) $x \geq -27$

10) $x < -13$

11) $22 \leq x$

12) $x > 4$

13) $x \geq 36$

14) $x > -25$

15) $x < -31$

16) $21 \leq x$

17) $x \leq 3$

18) $-4 \leq x$

19) $x > -7$

20) $x \leq 3$

21) $x < 2$

22) $x < -12$

23) $x > 36$

24) $108 \leq x$

25) $x < -24$

26) $x \geq 3$

27) $x \geq -5$

28) $x > 15$

29) $x \leq 8$

30) $x > 6$

31) $-7 < x$

Multi –Step Inequalities

1) $x \leq 5$

2) $x \geq 5$

3) $x \geq 9$

4) $x \leq 12$

5) $x \leq 9$

6) $x \leq 8$

7) $x \leq 9$

8) $x \leq 4$

9) $x \leq 8$

10) $x \geq 11$

11) $x \geq 9$

12) $x < 5$

13) $x \geq 25$

14) $x < -7$

15) $x \geq 15$

16) $x \geq 8$

17) $x > -8$

18) $x \leq -11$

19) $x \geq 12$

20) $x \geq 3$

21) $x \leq 5$

22) $x \leq -4$

23) $x < 9$

24) $x < 3$

25) $x < 7$

26) $x \geq 3$

Chapter 8: Lines and Slope

Math Topics that you'll learn in this Chapter:

- ✓ Finding Slope
- ✓ Graphing Lines Using Slope–Intercept Form
- ✓ Writing Linear Equations
- ✓ Graphing Linear Inequalities
- ✓ Finding Midpoint
- ✓ Finding Distance of Two Points

67

Finding Slope

✍️ *Find the slope of each line.*

1) $y = 2x - 8$, Slope $=$

2) $y = -6x + 3$, Slope $=$

3) $y = -x - 5$, Slope $=$

4) $y = -2x - 9$, Slope $=$

5) $y = 5 + 2x$, Slope $=$

6) $y = 1 - 8x$, Slope $=$

7) $y = -4x + 3$, Slope $=$

8) $y = -9x + 8$, Slope $=$

9) $y = -2x + 4$, Slope $=$

10) $y = 9x - 8$, Slope $=$

11) $y = \frac{1}{2}x + 4$, Slope $=$

12) $y = -\frac{2}{5}x + 7$, Slope $=$

13) $-x + 3y = 5$, Slope $=$

14) $4x + 4y = 6$, Slope $=$

15) $6y - 2x = 10$, Slope $=$

16) $3y - x = 2$, Slope $=$

✍️ *Find the slope of the line through each pair of points.*

17) $(4, 4), (8, 12)$, Slope $=$

23) $(8, 4), (9, 6)$, Slope $=$

18) $(-2, 4), (0, 6)$, Slope $=$

24) $(10, -1), (7, 8)$, Slope $=$

19) $(6, -2), (2, 6)$, Slope $=$

25) $(16, -3), (13, -6)$, Slope $=$

20) $(-4, -2), (0, 6)$, Slope $=$

26) $(12, 5), (8, 1)$, Slope $=$

21) $(6, 2), (3, 5)$, Slope $=$

27) $(6, 6), (8, 10)$, Slope $=$

22) $(-5, 1), (-1, 9)$, Slope $=$

28) $(10, -1), (8, 1)$, Slope $=$

Graphing Lines Using Slope–Intercept Form

✎ *Sketch the graph of each line.*

1) $y = -x + 1$

2) $y = 2x - 4$

3) $y = -x + 6$

4) $y = x - 4$

5) $y = 2x - 2$

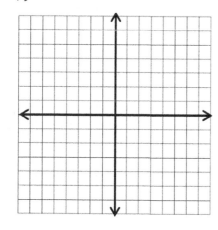

6) $y = -\frac{1}{2}x + 2$

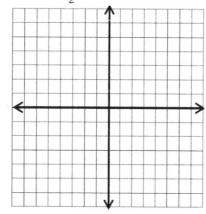

Writing Linear Equations

✍ *Write the equation of the line through the given points.*

1) through: $(2, -2), (3, 4)$ $y =$

2) through: $(-2, 4), (1, 7)$ $y =$

3) through: $(-1, 3), (3, 7)$ $y =$

4) through: $(6, 5), (3, 2)$ $y =$

5) through: $(7, -10), (2, 10)$ $y =$

6) through: $(7, 2), (6, 1)$ $y =$

7) through: $(6, -1), (4, 1)$ $y =$

8) through: $(-2, 8), (-4, -6)$ $y =$

9) through: $(-2, 5), (-3, 4)$ $y =$

10) through: $(6, 8), (8, -6)$ $y =$

11) through: $(-2, 5), (-4, -3)$ $y =$

12) through: $(8, 8), (4, -8)$ $y =$

13) through: $(7, -4)$, Slope: -1 $y =$

14) through: $(4, -10)$, Slope: -2 $y =$

15) through: $(6, 10)$, Slope: 9 $y =$

16) through: $(-6, 8)$, Slope: -2 $y =$

✍ *Solve each problem.*

17) What is the equation of a line with slope 6 and intercept 4? _____

18) What is the equation of a line with slope 5 and intercept 9? _____

19) What is the equation of a line with slope 8 and passes through point $(2, 8)$?

_____

20) What is the equation of a line with slope -3 and passes through point

$(-4, 10)$? _____

Finding Midpoint

✎ *Find the midpoint of the line segment with the given endpoints.*

1) $(4, 4), (0, 4),$ $midpoint = (\_\_, \_\_)$

2) $(5, 1), (-1, 5),$ $midpoint = (\_\_, \_\_)$

3) $(4, -2), (0, 6),$ $midpoint = (\_\_, \_\_)$

4) $(-3, 3), (-1, 5),$ $midpoint = (\_\_, \_\_)$

5) $(5, -2), (9, -6),$ $midpoint = (\_\_, \_\_)$

6) $(-6, -3), (4, -7),$ $midpoint = (\_\_, \_\_)$

7) $(7, 0), (-7, 8),$ $midpoint = (\_\_, \_\_)$

8) $(-8, 4), (-4, 0),$ $midpoint = (\_\_, \_\_)$

9) $(-3, 6), (9, -8),$ $midpoint = (\_\_, \_\_)$

10) $(6, 8), (6, -6),$ $midpoint = (\_\_, \_\_)$

11) $(6, 7), (-8, 5),$ $midpoint = (\_\_, \_\_)$

12) $(9, 3), (-3, -9),$ $midpoint = (\_\_, \_\_)$

13) $(-6, 12), (-4, 6),$ $midpoint = (\_\_, \_\_)$

14) $(10, 7), (8, -3),$ $midpoint = (\_\_, \_\_)$

15) $(13, 7), (-5, 3),$ $midpoint = (\_\_, \_\_)$

16) $(-9, -4), (-5, 8),$ $midpoint = (\_\_, \_\_)$

17) $(12, 5), (6, 15),$ $midpoint = (\_\_, \_\_)$

18) $(-6, -10), (12, -2),$ $midpoint = (\_\_, \_\_)$

19) $(14, 13), (-4, 9),$ $midpoint = (\_\_, \_\_)$

20) $(10, -4), (8, 12),$ $midpoint = (\_\_, \_\_)$

Finding Distance of Two Points

✏️ *Find the distance of each pair of points.*

1) $(0, 9), (4, 6),$

   Distance = ____

2) $(-4, 6), (8, 11),$

   Distance = ____

3) $(-6, 1), (-3, 5),$

   Distance = ____

4) $(-3, 2), (3, 10),$

   Distance = ____

5) $(-5, 3), (4, -9),$

   Distance = ____

6) $(-7, -5), (5, 0),$

   Distance = ____

7) $(4, 3), (-4, -12),$

   Distance = ____

8) $(10, 1), (-5, -19),$

   Distance = ____

9) $(3, 3), (-1, 5),$

   Distance = ____

10) $(2, -1), (10, 5),$

   Distance = ____

11) $(-3, 7), (-1, 4),$

   Distance = ____

12) $(5, -2), (9, -5),$

   Distance = ____

13) $(-8, 4), (4, 9),$

   Distance = ____

14) $(6, 8), (6, -6),$

   Distance = ____

15) $(6, -6), (0, 2),$

   Distance = ____

16) $(-4, 10), (-4, 4),$

   Distance = ____

17) $(-7, -6), (-2, 6),$

   Distance = ____

18) $(11, 0), (3, 15),$

   Distance = ____

Answers – Chapter 8

Finding Slope

1) 2

2) -6

3) -1

4) -2

5) 2

6) -8

7) -4

8) -9

9) -2

10) 9

11) $\frac{1}{2}$

12) $-\frac{2}{5}$

13) $\frac{1}{3}$

14) -1

15) $\frac{1}{3}$

16) $\frac{1}{3}$

17) 2

18) 1

19) -2

20) 2

21) -1

22) 2

23) 2

24) -3

25) 1

26) 1

27) 2

28) -1

Graphing Lines Using Slope–Intercept Form

1) $y = -x + 1$

2) $y = 2x - 4$

3) $y = -x + 6$

4) $y = x - 4$

5) $y = 2x - 2$

6) $y = -\frac{1}{2}x + 2$

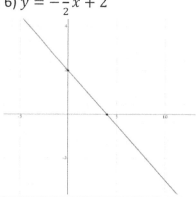

Writing Linear Equations

1) $y = 6x - 14$

2) $y = x + 6$

3) $y = x + 4$

4) $y = x - 1$

5) $y = -4x + 18$

6) $y = x - 5$

7) $y = -x + 5$

8) $y = 7x + 22$

9) $y = x + 7$

10) $y = -7x + 50$

11) $y = 4x + 13$

12) $y = 4x - 24$

13) $y = -x + 3$

14) $y = -2x - 2$

15) $y = 9x - 44$

16) $y = -2x - 4$

17) $y = 6x + 4$

18) $y = 5x + 9$

19) $y = 8x - 8$

20) $y = -3x - 2$

Finding Midpoint

1) $midpoint = (2, 4)$

2) $midpoint = (2, 3)$

3) $midpoint = (2, 2)$

4) $midpoint = (-2, 4)$

5) $midpoint = (7, -4)$

6) $midpoint = (-1, -5)$

7) $midpoint = (0, 4)$

8) $midpoint = (-6, 2)$

9) $midpoint = (3, -1)$

10) $midpoint = (6, 1)$

11) $midpoint = (-1, 6)$

12) $midpoint = (3, -3)$

13) $midpoint = (-5, 9)$

14) $midpoint = (9, 2)$

15) $midpoint = (4, 5)$

16) $midpoint = (-7, 2)$

17) $midpoint = (9, 10)$

18) $midpoint = (3, -6)$

19) $midpoint = (5, 11)$

20) $midpoint = (9, 4)$

Finding Distance of Two Points

1) Distance $= 5$

2) Distance $= 13$

3) Distance $= 5$

4) Distance $= 10$

5) Distance $= 15$

6) Distance $= 13$

7) Distance $= 17$

8) Distance $= 25$

9) Distance $= \sqrt{20} = 2\sqrt{5}$

10) Distance $= 10$

11) Distance $= \sqrt{13}$

12) Distance $= 5$

13) Distance $= 13$

14) Distance $= 14$

15) Distance $= 10$

16) Distance $= 6$

17) Distance $= 13$

18) Distance $= 17$

Chapter 9: Exponents and Variables

Math Topics that you'll learn in this Chapter:

- ✓ Multiplication Property of Exponents
- ✓ Division Property of Exponents
- ✓ Powers of Products and Quotients
- ✓ Zero and Negative Exponents
- ✓ Negative Exponents and Negative Bases
- ✓ Scientific Notation
- ✓ Radicals

Multiplication Property of Exponents

✎ *Simplify and write the answer in exponential form.*

1) $3 \times 3^2 =$

2) $4^3 \times 4 =$

3) $2^2 \times 2^2 =$

4) $6^2 \times 6^2 =$

5) $7^3 \times 7^2 \times 7 =$

6) $2 \times 2^2 \times 2^2 =$

7) $5^3 \times 5^2 \times 5 \times 5 =$

8) $2x \times x =$

9) $x^3 \times x^2 =$

10) $x^4 \times x^4 =$

11) $x^2 \times x^2 \times x^2 =$

12) $6x \times 6x =$

13) $2x^2 \times 2x^2 =$

14) $3x^2 \times x =$

15) $4x^4 \times 4x^4 \times 4x^4 =$

16) $2x^2 \times x^2 =$

17) $x^4 \times 3x =$

18) $x \times 2x^2 =$

19) $5x^4 \times 5x^4 =$

20) $2yx^2 \times 2x =$

21) $3x^4 \times y^2x^4 =$

22) $y^2x^3 \times y^5x^2 =$

23) $4yx^3 \times 2x^2y^3 =$

24) $6x^2 \times 6x^3y^4 =$

25) $3x^4y^5 \times 7x^2y^3 =$

26) $7x^2y^5 \times 9xy^3 =$

27) $7xy^4 \times 4x^3y^3 =$

28) $3x^5y^3 \times 8x^2y^3 =$

29) $6x \times y^5x^2 \times y^3 =$

30) $yx^3 \times 3y^3x^2 \times 2xy =$

31) $5yx^3 \times 4y^2x \times xy^3 =$

32) $6x^2 \times 3x^3y^4 \times 10yx^3 =$

Division Property of Exponents

✍ *Simplify and write the answer.*

1) $\dfrac{3^2}{3^3} =$

2) $\dfrac{2^6}{2^2} =$

3) $\dfrac{4^4}{4} =$

4) $\dfrac{5}{5^4} =$

5) $\dfrac{x}{x^3} =$

6) $\dfrac{3 \times 3^3}{3^2 \times 3^4} =$

7) $\dfrac{5^8}{5^3} =$

8) $\dfrac{5 \times 5^6}{5^2 \times 5^7} =$

9) $\dfrac{3^4 \times 3^7}{3^2 \times 3^8} =$

10) $\dfrac{5x}{10x^3} =$

11) $\dfrac{5x^3}{2x^5} =$

12) $\dfrac{18x^3}{14x^6} =$

13) $\dfrac{12x^3}{8xy^8} =$

14) $\dfrac{24xy^3}{4x^4y^2} =$

15) $\dfrac{21x^3y^9}{7xy^5} =$

16) $\dfrac{36x^2y^9}{4x^3} =$

17) $\dfrac{18x^3y^4}{10x^6y^8} =$

18) $\dfrac{16y^2x^{14}}{24yx^8} =$

19) $\dfrac{15x^4y}{9x^9y^2} =$

20) $\dfrac{7x^7y^2}{28x^5y^6} =$

Powers of Products and Quotients

✎ *Simplify and write the answer.*

1) $(3^2)^2 =$

2) $(5^2)^3 =$

3) $(3 \times 3^3)^4 =$

4) $(6 \times 6^4)^2 =$

5) $(3^3 \times 3^2)^3 =$

6) $(5^4 \times 5^5)^2 =$

7) $(2 \times 2^4)^2 =$

8) $(2x^6)^2 =$

9) $(11x^5)^2 =$

10) $(4x^2y^4)^4 =$

11) $(2x^4y^4)^3 =$

12) $(3x^2y^2)^2 =$

13) $(3x^4y^3)^4 =$

14) $(2x^6y^8)^2 =$

15) $(12x^3x)^3 =$

16) $(5x^9x^6)^3 =$

17) $(5x^{10}y^3)^3 =$

18) $(14x^3x^3)^2 =$

19) $(3x^35x)^2 =$

20) $(10x^{11}y^3)^2 =$

21) $(9x^7y^5)^2 =$

22) $(4x^4y^6)^5 =$

23) $(3x4y^3)^2 =$

24) $\left(\frac{6x}{x^2}\right)^2 =$

25) $\left(\frac{x^5y^5}{x^2y^2}\right)^3 =$

26) $\left(\frac{24x}{4x^6}\right)^2 =$

27) $\left(\frac{x^5}{x^6y^2}\right)^2 =$

28) $\left(\frac{xy^3}{x^2y^5}\right)^3 =$

29) $\left(\frac{3xy^3}{x^4}\right)^2 =$

30) $\left(\frac{xy^5}{4xy^3}\right)^3 =$

Chapter 9: Exponents and Variables

Zero and Negative Exponents

✎ *Evaluate the following expressions.*

1) $2^{-1} =$

2) $3^{-2} =$

3) $0^{10} =$

4) $1^{-8} =$

5) $8^{-1} =$

6) $8^{-2} =$

7) $2^{-4} =$

8) $10^{-2} =$

9) $9^{-2} =$

10) $3^{-3} =$

11) $7^{-3} =$

12) $3^{-4} =$

13) $6^{-3} =$

14) $5^{-3} =$

15) $22^{-1} =$

16) $4^{-4} =$

17) $5^{-4} =$

18) $15^{-2} =$

19) $4^{-5} =$

20) $9^{-3} =$

21) $3^{-5} =$

22) $5^{-4} =$

23) $12^{-2} =$

24) $15^{-3} =$

25) $20^{-3} =$

26) $50^{-2} =$

27) $18^{-3} =$

28) $24^{-2} =$

29) $30^{-3} =$

30) $10^{-5} =$

31) $\left(\frac{1}{8}\right)^{-1} =$

32) $\left(\frac{1}{5}\right)^{-2} =$

33) $\left(\frac{1}{7}\right)^{-2} =$

34) $\left(\frac{2}{3}\right)^{-2} =$

35) $\left(\frac{1}{5}\right)^{-3} =$

36) $\left(\frac{3}{4}\right)^{-2} =$

37) $\left(\frac{2}{5}\right)^{-2} =$

38) $\left(\frac{1}{2}\right)^{-8} =$

39) $\left(\frac{2}{3}\right)^{-3} =$

40) $\left(\frac{3}{4}\right)^{-3} =$

41) $\left(\frac{5}{6}\right)^{-2} =$

42) $\left(\frac{6}{9}\right)^{-2} =$

Negative Exponents and Negative Bases

✎ *Simplify and write the answer.*

1) $-2^{-1} =$

2) $-4^{-2} =$

3) $-3^{-4} =$

4) $-x^{-5} =$

5) $2x^{-1} =$

6) $-4x^{-3} =$

7) $-12x^{-5} =$

8) $-5x^{-2}y^{-3} =$

9) $20x^{-4}y^{-1} =$

10) $14a^{-6}b^{-7} =$

11) $-12x^2y^{-3} =$

12) $-\dfrac{25}{x^{-6}} =$

13) $-\dfrac{2x}{y^{-4}} =$

14) $\left(-\dfrac{1}{3x}\right)^{-2} =$

15) $\left(-\dfrac{3}{4x}\right)^{-2} =$

16) $-\dfrac{9}{a^{-7}b^{-2}} =$

17) $-\dfrac{5x}{x^{-3}} =$

18) $-\dfrac{a^{-3}}{b^{-2}} =$

19) $-\dfrac{8}{x^{-3}} =$

20) $\dfrac{5b}{-9c^{-4}} =$

21) $\dfrac{9ab}{a^{-3}b^{-1}} =$

22) $-\dfrac{15a^{-2}}{30b^{-3}} =$

23) $\dfrac{4ab^{-2}}{-3c^{-2}} =$

24) $\left(\dfrac{3a}{2c}\right)^{-2} =$

25) $\left(-\dfrac{3x}{4yz}\right)^{-2} =$

26) $\dfrac{15ab^{-6}}{-9c^{-2}} =$

27) $\left(-\dfrac{x^3}{x^4}\right)^{-3} =$

28) $\left(-\dfrac{x^{-2}}{2x^2}\right)^{-2} =$

Scientific Notation

✎ *Write each number in scientific notation.*

1) $0.114 =$

2) $0.06 =$

3) $8.6 =$

4) $30 =$

5) $60 =$

6) $0.004 =$

7) $78 =$

8) $1,600 =$

9) $1,450 =$

10) $31,000 =$

11) $2,000,000 =$

12) $0.0000003 =$

13) $554,000 =$

14) $0.000725 =$

15) $0.00034 =$

16) $86,000,000 =$

17) $62,000 =$

18) $97,000,000 =$

19) $0.0000045 =$

20) $0.0019 =$

✎ *Write each number in standard notation.*

21) $2 \times 10^{-1} =$

22) $8 \times 10^{-2} =$

23) $1.8 \times 10^3 =$

24) $9 \times 10^{-4} =$

25) $1.7 \times 10^{-2} =$

26) $9 \times 10^3 =$

27) $6 \times 10^4 =$

28) $2.18 \times 10^5 =$

29) $5 \times 10^{-3} =$

30) $9.4 \times 10^{-5} =$

Chapter 9: Exponents and Variables

Radicals

✏️ *Simplify and write the answer.*

1) $\sqrt{1} =$ ____

2) $\sqrt{0} =$ ____

3) $\sqrt{16} =$ ____

4) $\sqrt{4} =$ ____

5) $\sqrt{9} =$ ____

6) $\sqrt{25} =$ ____

7) $\sqrt{49} =$ ____

8) $\sqrt{36} =$ ____

9) $\sqrt{64} =$ ____

10) $\sqrt{81} =$ ____

11) $\sqrt{121} =$ ____

12) $\sqrt{225} =$ ____

13) $\sqrt{144} =$ ____

14) $\sqrt{100} =$ ____

15) $\sqrt{256} =$ ____

16) $\sqrt{289} =$ ____

17) $\sqrt{324} =$ ____

18) $\sqrt{400} =$ ____

19) $\sqrt{900} =$ ____

20) $\sqrt{529} =$ ____

21) $\sqrt{361} =$ ____

22) $\sqrt{169} =$ ____

23) $\sqrt{196} =$ ____

24) $\sqrt{90} =$ ____

✏️ *Evaluate.*

25) $\sqrt{6} \times \sqrt{6} =$

26) $\sqrt{5} \times \sqrt{5} =$

27) $\sqrt{8} \times \sqrt{8} =$

28) $\sqrt{2} + \sqrt{2} =$

29) $\sqrt{8} + \sqrt{8} =$

30) $6\sqrt{5} - 2\sqrt{5} =$

31) $\sqrt{25} \times \sqrt{16} =$

32) $\sqrt{25} \times \sqrt{64} =$

33) $\sqrt{64} \times \sqrt{49} =$

34) $5\sqrt{5} \times 3\sqrt{5} =$

35) $7\sqrt{3} \times 2\sqrt{3} =$

36) $5\sqrt{2} - \sqrt{8} =$

Answers – Chapter 9

Multiplication Property of Exponents

1) 3^3

2) 4^4

3) 2^4

4) 6^4

5) 7^6

6) 2^5

7) 5^7

8) $2x^2$

9) x^5

10) x^8

11) x^6

12) $36x^2$

13) $4x^4$

14) $3x^3$

15) $64x^{12}$

16) $2x^4$

17) $3x^5$

18) $2x^3$

19) $25x^8$

20) $4x^3y$

21) $3x^8y^2$

22) x^5y^7

23) $8x^5y^4$

24) $36x^5y^4$

25) $21x^6y^8$

26) $63x^3y^8$

27) $28x^4y^7$

28) $24x^7y^6$

29) $6x^3y^8$

30) $6x^6y^5$

31) $20x^5y^6$

32) $180x^8y^5$

Division Property of Exponents

1) $\frac{1}{3}$

2) 2^4

3) 4^3

4) $\frac{1}{5^3}$

5) $\frac{1}{x^2}$

6) $\frac{1}{3^2}$

7) 5^5

8) $\frac{1}{5^2}$

9) 3

10) $\frac{1}{2x^2}$

11) $\frac{5}{2x^2}$

12) $\frac{9}{7x^3}$

13) $\frac{3x^2}{2y^8}$

14) $\frac{6y}{x^3}$

15) $3x^2y^4$

16) $\frac{9y^9}{x}$

17) $\frac{9}{5x^3y^4}$

18) $\frac{2yx^6}{3}$

19) $\frac{5}{3x^5y}$

20) $\frac{x^2}{4y^4}$

Powers of Products and Quotients

1) 3^4

2) 5^6

3) 3^{16}

4) 6^{10}

5) 3^{15}

6) 5^{18}

7) 2^{10}

8) $4x^{12}$

9) $121x^{10}$

10) $256x^8y^{16}$

11) $8x^{12}y^{12}$

12) $9x^4y^4$

13) $81x^{16}y^{12}$

14) $4x^{12}y^{16}$

15) $1,728x^{12}$

16) $125x^{45}$

17) $125x^{30}y^9$

18) $196x^{12}$

19) $225x^8$

20) $100x^{22}y^6$

21) $81x^{14}y^{10}$

22) $1,024x^{20}y^{30}$

23) $144x^2y^6$

24) $\dfrac{36}{x^2}$

25) x^9y^9

26) $\dfrac{36}{x^{10}}$

27) $\dfrac{1}{x^2y^4}$

28) $\dfrac{1}{x^3y^6}$

29) $\dfrac{9y^6}{x^6}$

30) $\dfrac{y^6}{64}$

Zero and Negative Exponents

1) $\frac{1}{2}$

2) $\frac{1}{9}$

3) 0

4) 1

5) $\frac{1}{8}$

6) $\frac{1}{64}$

7) $\frac{1}{16}$

8) $\frac{1}{100}$

9) $\frac{1}{81}$

10) $\frac{1}{27}$

11) $\frac{1}{343}$

12) $\frac{1}{81}$

13) $\frac{1}{216}$

14) $\frac{1}{125}$

15) $\frac{1}{22}$

16) $\frac{1}{256}$

17) $\frac{1}{625}$

18) $\frac{1}{225}$

19) $\frac{1}{1,024}$

20) $\frac{1}{729}$

21) $\frac{1}{243}$

22) $\frac{1}{625}$

23) $\frac{1}{144}$

24) $\frac{1}{3,375}$

25) $\frac{1}{8,000}$

26) $\frac{1}{2,500}$

27) $\frac{1}{5,832}$

28) $\frac{1}{576}$

29) $\frac{1}{27,000}$

30) $\frac{1}{100,000}$

31) 8

32) 25

33) 49

34) $\frac{9}{4}$

35) 125

36) $\frac{16}{9}$

37) $\frac{25}{4}$

38) 256

39) $\frac{27}{8}$

40) $\frac{64}{27}$

41) $\frac{36}{25}$

42) $\frac{81}{36}$

Negative Exponents and Negative Bases

1) $-\dfrac{1}{2}$

2) $-\dfrac{1}{16}$

3) $-\dfrac{1}{81}$

4) $-\dfrac{1}{x^5}$

5) $\dfrac{2}{x}$

6) $-\dfrac{4}{x^3}$

7) $-\dfrac{12}{x^5}$

8) $-\dfrac{5}{x^2y^3}$

9) $\dfrac{20}{x^4y}$

10) $\dfrac{14}{a^6b^7}$

11) $-\dfrac{12x^2}{y^3}$

12) $-25x^6$

13) $-2xy^4$

14) $9x^2$

15) $\dfrac{16x^2}{9}$

16) $-9a^7b^2$

17) $-5x^4$

18) $-\dfrac{b^2}{a^3}$

19) $-8x^3$

20) $-\dfrac{5bc^4}{9}$

21) $9a^4b^2$

22) $-\dfrac{b^3}{2a^2}$

23) $-\dfrac{4ac^2}{3b^2}$

24) $\dfrac{4c^2}{9a^2}$

25) $\dfrac{16y^2z^2}{9x^2}$

26) $-\dfrac{5ac^2}{3b^6}$

27) $-x^3$

28) $4x^8$

Scientific Notation

1) 1.14×10^{-1}

2) 6×10^{-2}

3) 8.6×10^{0}

4) 3×10^{1}

5) 6×10^{1}

6) 4×10^{-3}

7) 7.8×10^{1}

8) 1.6×10^{3}

9) 1.45×10^{3}

10) 3.1×10^{4}

11) 2×10^{6}

12) 3×10^{-7}

13) 5.54×10^{5}

14) 7.25×10^{-4}

15) 3.4×10^{-4}

16) 8.6×10^{7}

17) 6.2×10^{4}

18) 9.7×10^{7}

19) 4.5×10^{-6}

20) 1.9×10^{-3}

21) 0.2

22) 0.08

23) $1,800$

24) 0.0009

25) 0.017

26) $9,000$

27) $60,000$

28) $218,000$

29) 0.005

30) 0.000094

Radicals

1) 1	13) 12	25) 6
2) 0	14) 10	26) 5
3) 4	15) 16	27) 8
4) 2	16) 17	28) $2\sqrt{2}$
5) 3	17) 18	29) $2\sqrt{8} = 4\sqrt{2}$
6) 5	18) 20	30) $4\sqrt{5}$
7) 7	19) 30	31) 20
8) 6	20) 23	32) 40
9) 8	21) 19	33) 56
10) 9	22) 13	34) 75
11) 11	23) 14	35) 42
12) 15	24) $3\sqrt{10}$	36) $3\sqrt{2}$

Chapter 10:
Polynomials

Math Topics that you'll learn in this Chapter:

- ✓ Simplifying Polynomials
- ✓ Adding and Subtracting Polynomials
- ✓ Multiplying Monomials
- ✓ Multiplying and Dividing Monomials
- ✓ Multiplying a Polynomial and a Monomial
- ✓ Multiplying Binomials
- ✓ Factoring Trinomials

Simplifying Polynomials

✏️ *Simplify each expression.*

1) $3(2x + 1) =$ _____

2) $2(4x - 6) =$ _____

3) $4(3x + 3) =$ _____

4) $2(4x + 5) =$ _____

5) $-3(8x - 7) =$ _____

6) $2x(3x + 4) =$ _____

7) $3x^2 + 3x^2 - 2x^3 =$ _____

8) $2x - x^2 + 6x^3 + 4 =$ _____

9) $5x + 2x^2 - 9x^3 =$ _____

10) $7x^2 + 5x^4 - 2x^3 =$ _____

11) $-3x^2 + 5x^3 + 6x^4 =$ _____

12) $(x - 3)(x - 4) =$ _____

13) $(x - 5)(x + 4) =$ _____

14) $(x - 6)(x - 3) =$ _____

15) $(2x + 5)(x + 8) =$ _____

16) $(3x - 8)(x + 4) =$ _____

17) $-8x^2 + 2x^3 - 10x^4 + 5x =$ _____

18) $11 - 6x^2 + 5x^2 - 12x^3 + 22 =$ _____

19) $3x^2 - 4x + 4x^3 + 10x - 21x =$ _____

20) $10 - 6x^2 + 5x^2 - 3x^3 + 2 =$ _____

21) $3x^5 - 2x^3 + 8x^2 - x^5 =$ _____

22) $(5x^3 - 1) + (4x^3 - 6x^3) =$ _____

Adding and Subtracting Polynomials

✎ *Add or subtract expressions.*

1) $(x^2 - 5) + (x^2 + 6) = $ _____

2) $(2x^2 - 6) - (3 - 2x^2) = $ _____

3) $(x^3 + 3x^2) - (x^3 + 6) = $ _____

4) $(4x^3 - x^2) + (6x^2 - 8x) = $ _____

5) $(2x^3 + 3x) - (5x^3 + 2) = $ _____

6) $(5x^3 - 2) + (2x^3 + 10) = $ _____

7) $(7x^3 + 5) - (9 - 4x^3) = $ _____

8) $(5x^2 + 3x^3) - (2x^3 + 6) = $ _____

9) $(8x^2 - x) + (4x - 8x^2) = $ _____

10) $(6x + 9x^2) - (5x + 2) = $ _____

11) $(7x^4 - 2x) - (6x - 2x^4) = $ _____

12) $(2x - 4x^3) - (9x^3 + 6x) = $ _____

13) $(8x^3 - 8x^2) - (6x^2 - 3x) = $ _____

14) $(9x^2 - 6) + (5x^2 - 4x^3) = $ _____

15) $(8x^3 + 3x^4) - (x^4 - 3x^3) = $ _____

16) $(-4x^3 - 2x) + (5x - 2x^3) = $ _____

17) $(9x - 5x^4) - (8x^4 + 4x) = $ _____

18) $(8x - 3x^2) - (7x^4 - 3x^2) = $ _____

19) $(9x^3 - 7) + (5x^3 - 4x^2) = $ _____

20) $(7x^3 + x^4) - (6x^4 - 5x^3) = $ _____

Chapter 10: Polynomials

Multiplying Monomials

✎ *Simplify each expression.*

1) $4x^7 \times x^3 =$

2) $6y^2 \times 6y^3 =$

3) $-6z^7 \times 4z^4 =$

4) $5x^5y \times 8xy^3 =$

5) $-6xy^8 \times 3x^5y^3 =$

6) $7a^4b^2 \times 3a^8b =$

7) $5xy^5 \times 3x^3y^4 =$

8) $5p^5q^4 \times (-6pq^4) =$

9) $8s^6t^2 \times 6s^3t^7 =$

10) $(-8x^5y^2) \times 4x^6y^3 =$

11) $9xy^6z \times 3y^4z^2 =$

12) $12x^5y^4 \times 2x^8y =$

13) $4pq^5 \times (-7p^4q^8) =$

14) $9s^4t^2 \times (-5st^5) =$

15) $10p^3q^5 \times (-4p^4q^6) =$

16) $(-5p^2q^4r) \times 7pq^5r^3 =$

17) $(-9a^4b^7c^4) \times (-4a^7b) =$

18) $7u^5v^9 \times (-5u^{12}v^7) =$

19) $4u^4v^9z^2 \times (-5uv^8z) =$

20) $(-6xy^3z^5) \times 3x^3yz^7 =$

21) $6x^2y^3z^5 \times (-7x^4y^2z) =$

22) $7a^5b^8c^{12} \times 4a^6b^5c^9 =$

www.EffortlessMath.com

Multiplying and Dividing Monomials

✎ *Simplify each expression.*

1) $(3x^5)(2x^2) =$ _____

2) $(6x^5)(2x^4) =$ _____

3) $(-7x^9)(2x^5) =$ _____

4) $(7x^7y^9)(-5x^6y^6) =$ _____

5) $(8x^5y^6)(3x^2y^5) =$ _____

6) $(8yx^2)(7y^5x^3) =$ _____

7) $(4x^2y)(2x^2y^3) =$ _____

8) $(-2x^9y^4)(-9x^6y^8) =$ _____

9) $(-5x^8y^2)(-6x^4y^5) =$ _____

10) $(8x^8y)(-7x^4y^3) =$ _____

11) $(9x^6y^2)(6x^7y^4) =$

12) $(8x^9y^5)(6x^5y^4) =$ _____

13) $(-5x^8y^9)(7x^7y^8) =$ _____

14) $(6x^2y^5)(5x^3y^2) =$ _____

15) $(9x^5y^{12})(4x^7y^9) =$ _____

16) $(-10x^{14}y^8)(2x^7y^5) =$ _____

17) $\frac{6x^5y^7}{xy^6} =$ _____

18) $\frac{9x^6y^6}{3x^4y} =$ _____

19) $\frac{16x^4y^6}{4xy} =$ _____

20) $\frac{-30x^9y^8}{5x^5y^4} =$ _____

Multiplying a Polynomial and a Monomial

✏️ *Find each product.*

1) $x(x - 5) =$

_____

2) $2(3 + x) =$

_____

3) $x(x - 7) =$

_____

4) $x(x + 9) =$

_____

5) $2x(x - 2) =$

_____

6) $5(4x + 3) =$

_____

7) $4x(3x - 4) =$

_____

8) $x(5x + 2y) =$

_____

9) $3x(x - 2y) =$

_____

10) $6x(3x - 4y) =$

_____

11) $2x(3x - 8) =$

_____

12) $6x(4x - 6y) =$

_____

13) $3x(4x - 2y) =$

_____

14) $2x(2x - 6y) =$

_____

15) $5x(x^2 + y^2) =$

_____

16) $3x(2x^2 - y^2) =$

_____

17) $6(9x^2 + 3y^2) =$

_____

18) $4x(-3x^2y + 2y) =$

_____

19) $-3(6x^2 - 5xy + 3) =$

_____

20) $6(x^2 - 4xy - 3) =$

_____

Multiplying Binomials

✎ *Find each product.*

1) $(x - 3)(x + 4) =$

_____

2) $(x + 3)(x + 5) =$

_____

3) $(x - 6)(x - 7) =$

_____

4) $(x - 9)(x - 4) =$

_____

5) $(x - 7)(x - 5) =$

_____

6) $(x + 6)(x + 2) =$

_____

7) $(x - 9)(x + 3) =$

_____

8) $(x - 8)(x - 5) =$

_____

9) $(x + 3)(x + 7) =$

_____

10) $(x - 9)(x + 4) =$

_____

11) $(x + 6)(x + 6) =$

_____

12) $(x + 7)(x + 7) =$

_____

13) $(x - 8)(x + 7) =$

_____

14) $(x + 9)(x + 9) =$

_____

15) $(x - 8)(x - 8) =$

_____

16) $(x - 9)(x + 5) =$

_____

17) $(2x - 5)(x + 4) =$

_____

18) $(2x + 6)(x + 3) =$

_____

19) $(2x + 4)(x + 5) =$

_____

20) $(2x - 3)(2x + 2) =$

_____

Factoring Trinomials

✎ *Factor each trinomial.*

1) $x^2 + 5x + 4 =$

_____

2) $x^2 + 5x + 6 =$

_____

3) $x^2 - 4x + 3 =$

_____

4) $x^2 - 10x + 25 =$

_____

5) $x^2 - 13x + 40 =$

_____

6) $x^2 + 8x + 12 =$

_____

7) $x^2 - 6x - 27 =$

_____

8) $x^2 - 14x + 48 =$

_____

9) $x^2 + 15x + 56 =$

_____

10) $x^2 - 5x - 36 =$

_____

11) $x^2 + 12x + 36 =$

_____

12) $x^2 + 16x + 63 =$

_____

13) $x^2 + x - 72 =$

_____

14) $x^2 + 18x + 81 =$

_____

15) $x^2 - 16x + 64 =$

_____

16) $x^2 - 18x + 81 =$

_____

17) $2x^2 + 10x + 8 =$

_____

18) $2x^2 + 4x - 6 =$

_____

19) $2x^2 + 9x + 4 =$

_____

20) $4x^2 + 4x - 24 =$

_____

Answers – Chapter 10

Simplifying Polynomials

1) $6x + 3$

2) $8x - 12$

3) $12x + 12$

4) $8x + 10$

5) $-24x + 21$

6) $6x^2 + 8x$

7) $-2x^3 + 6x^2$

8) $6x^3 - x^2 + 2x + 4$

9) $-9x^3 + 2x^2 + 5x$

10) $5x^4 - 2x^3 + 7x^2$

11) $6x^4 + 5x^3 - 3x^2$

12) $x^2 - 7x + 12$

13) $x^2 - x - 20$

14) $x^2 - 9x + 18$

15) $2x^2 + 21x + 40$

16) $3x^2 + 4x - 32$

17) $-10x^4 + 2x^3 - 8x^2 + 5x$

18) $-12x^3 - x^2 + 33$

19) $4x^3 + 3x^2 - 15x$

20) $-3x^3 - x^2 + 12$

21) $2x^5 - 2x^3 + 8x^2$

22) $3x^3 - 1$

Adding and Subtracting Polynomials

1) $2x^2 + 1$

2) $4x^2 - 9$

3) $3x^2 - 6$

4) $4x^3 + 5x^2 - 8x$

5) $-3x^3 + 3x - 2$

6) $7x^3 + 8$

7) $11x^3 - 4$

8) $x^3 + 5x^2 - 6$

9) $3x$

10) $9x^2 + x - 2$

11) $9x^4 - 8x$

12) $-13x^3 - 4x$

13) $8x^3 - 14x^2 + 3x$

14) $-4x^3 + 14x^2 - 6$

15) $2x^4 + 11x^3$

16) $-6x^3 + 3x$

17) $-13x^4 + 5x$

18) $-7x^4 + 8x$

19) $14x^3 - 4x^2 - 7$

20) $-5x^4 + 12x^3$

Multiplying Monomials

1) $4x^{10}$

2) $36y^5$

3) $-24z^{11}$

4) $40x^6y^4$

5) $-18x^6y^{11}$

6) $21a^{12}b^3$

7) $15x^4y^9$

8) $-30p^6q^8$

9) $48s^9t^9$

10) $-32x^{11}y^5$

11) $27xy^{10}z^3$

12) $24x^{13}y^5$

13) $-28p^5q^{13}$

14) $-45s^5t^7$

15) $-40p^7q^{11}$

16) $-35p^3q^9r^4$

17) $36a^{11}b^8c^4$

18) $-35u^{17}v^{16}$

19) $-20u^5v^{17}z^3$

20) $-18x^4y^4z^{12}$

21) $-42x^6y^5z^6$

22) $28a^{11}b^{13}c^{21}$

Multiplying and Dividing Monomials

1) $6x^7$

2) $12x^9$

3) $-14x^{14}$

4) $-35x^{13}y^{15}$

5) $24x^7y^{11}$

6) $56y^6x^5$

7) $8x^4y^4$

8) $18x^{15}y^{12}$

9) $30x^{12}y^7$

10) $-56x^{12}y^4$

11) $54x^{13}y^6$

12) $48x^{14}y^9$

13) $-35x^{15}y^{17}$

14) $30x^5y^7$

15) $36x^{12}y^{21}$

16) $-20x^{21}y^{13}$

17) $6x^4y$

18) $3x^2y^5$

19) $4x^3y^5$

20) $-6x^4y^4$

Multiplying a Polynomial and a Monomial

1) $x^2 - 5x$

2) $2x + 6$

3) $x^2 - 7x$

4) $x^2 + 9x$

5) $2x^2 - 4x$

6) $20x + 15$

7) $12x^2 - 16x$

8) $5x^2 + 2xy$

9) $3x^2 - 6xy$

10) $18x^2 - 24xy$

11) $6x^2 - 16x$

12) $24x^2 - 36xy$

13) $12x^2 - 6xy$

14) $4x^2 - 12xy$

15) $5x^3 + 5xy^2$

16) $6x^3 - 3xy^2$

17) $54x^2 + 18y^2$

18) $-12x^3y + 8xy$

19) $-18x^2 + 15xy - 9$

20) $6x^2 - 24xy - 18$

Multiplying Binomials

1) $x^2 + x - 12$

2) $x^2 + 8x + 15$

3) $x^2 - 13x + 42$

4) $x^2 - 13x + 36$

5) $x^2 - 12x + 35$

6) $x^2 + 8x + 12$

7) $x^2 - 6x - 27$

8) $x^2 - 13x + 40$

9) $x^2 + 10x + 21$

10) $x^2 - 5x - 36$

11) $x^2 + 12x + 36$

12) $x^2 + 14x + 49$

13) $x^2 - x - 56$

14) $x^2 + 18x + 81$

15) $x^2 - 16x + 64$

16) $x^2 - 4x - 45$

17) $2x^2 + 3x - 20$

18) $2x^2 + 12x + 18$

19) $2x^2 + 14x + 20$

20) $4x^2 - 2x - 6$

Factoring Trinomials

1) $(x + 4)(x + 1)$

2) $(x + 3)(x + 2)$

3) $(x - 1)(x - 3)$

4) $(x - 5)(x - 5)$

5) $(x - 8)(x - 5)$

6) $(x + 6)(x + 2)$

7) $(x - 9)(x + 3)$

8) $(x - 8)(x - 6)$

9) $(x + 8)(x + 7)$

10) $(x - 9)(x + 4)$

11) $(x + 6)(x + 6)$

12) $(x + 7)(x + 9)$

13) $(x - 8)(x + 9)$

14) $(x + 9)(x + 9)$

15) $(x - 8)(x - 8)$

16) $(x - 9)(x - 9)$

17) $2(x + 1)(x + 4)$

18) $2(x - 1)(x + 3)$

19) $(2x + 1)(x + 4)$

20) $(2x - 4)(2x + 6)$

Chapter 11: Geometry and Solid Figures

Math Topics that you'll learn in this Chapter:

- ✓ The Pythagorean Theorem
- ✓ Triangles
- ✓ Polygons
- ✓ Circles
- ✓ Trapezoids
- ✓ Cubes
- ✓ Rectangle Prisms
- ✓ Cylinder

105

The Pythagorean Theorem

✎ *Do the following lengths form a right triangle?*

1) _____

2) _____

3) _____

4) _____

5) _____

6) _____

7) _____

8) _____

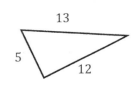

✎ *Find the missing side.*

9) _____

10) _____

11) _____

12) _____

13) _____

14) _____

15) _____

16) _____

Triangles

✏️ *Find the measure of the unknown angle in each triangle.*

1) _____

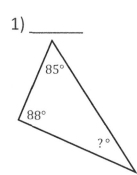

85°
88°
?°

2) _____

55°
70°
?°

3) _____

62°
75°
?°

4) _____

55°
70°
?°

5) _____

55°
80°
?°

6) _____

60°
74°
?°
?°

7) _____

?°
43°
85°

8) _____

35°
74° ?°

✏️ *Find area of each triangle.*

9) _____

6
11
9

10) _____

12
13
9

11) _____

14 cm
9 cm
16 cm

12) _____

12 in
8 in
18 in

Polygons

✏️ *Find the perimeter of each shape.*

1) (square) _____   2) _____   3) _____   4) (square) _____

6 cm

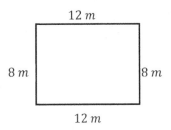

12 m

8 m   8 m

12 m

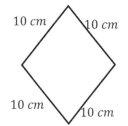

10 cm   10 cm

10 cm   10 cm

8 m

5) (regular hexagon)   6) _____   7) (parallelogram)   8) (regular hexagon)

_____   _____   _____

16 m

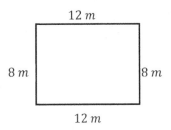

14 m

12 m   12 m

18 m

6 cm

8 cm

20 ft

9) _____   10) _____   11) _____   12) (regular hexagon)

_____

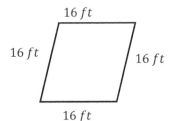

16 ft

16 ft   16 ft

16 ft

22 in

18 in   18 in

22 in

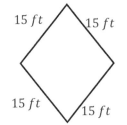

15 ft   15 ft

15 ft   15 ft

30 in

Circles

✍ **Find the Circumference of each circle.** ($\pi = 3.14$)

1) ____   2) ____   3) ____   4) ____   5) ____   6) ____

7) ____   8) ____   9) ____   10) ____   11) ____   12) ____

✍ **Complete the table below.** ($\pi = 3.14$)

	Radius	Diameter	Circumference	Area
Circle 1	2 inches	4 inches	12.56 inches	12.56 square inches
Circle 2		8 meters		
Circle 3				113.04 square feet
Circle 4			50.24 miles	
Circle 5		9 kilometers		
Circle 6	7 centimeters			
Circle 7		18 feet		
Circle 8				78.5 square meters
Circle 9			69.08 inches	
Circle 10	10 feet			

Cubes

✍ *Find the volume of each cube.*

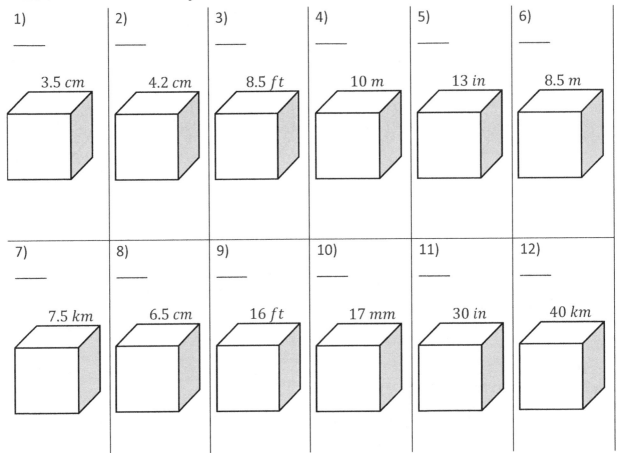

1)	2)	3)	4)	5)	6)
3.5 cm	4.2 cm	8.5 ft	10 m	13 in	8.5 m

7)	8)	9)	10)	11)	12)
7.5 km	6.5 cm	16 ft	17 mm	30 in	40 km

✍ *Find the surface area of each cube.*

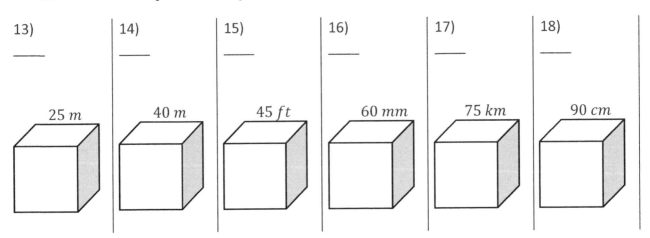

13)	14)	15)	16)	17)	18)
25 m	40 m	45 ft	60 mm	75 km	90 cm

Trapezoids

✏️ *Find the area of each trapezoid.*

1) _____

12 cm
8 cm
14 cm

2) _____

16 m
12 m
20 m

3) _____

8 ft
6 ft
10 ft

4) _____

9 cm
6 cm
12 cm

5) _____

4 cm
6 cm
12 cm

6) _____

12 in
8 in
16 in

7) _____

20 cm
16 cm
24 cm

8) _____

18 in
14 in
22 in

✏️ *Solve.*

9) A trapezoid has an area of 78 cm^2 and its height is 10 cm and one base is 8 cm. What is the other base length? _____

10) If a trapezoid has an area of 160 ft^2 and the lengths of the bases are 12 ft and 8 ft, find the height. _____

11) If a trapezoid has an area of 180 m^2 and its height is 8 m and one base is 10 m, find the other base length. _____

12) The area of a trapezoid is 150 ft^2 and its height is 20 ft. If one base of the trapezoid is 12 ft, what is the other base length? _____

Rectangular Prisms

✎ *Find the volume of each Rectangular Prism.*

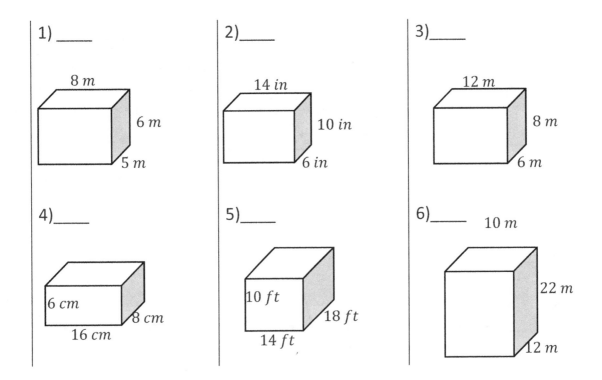

1) ____

8 m
6 m
5 m

2) ____

14 in
10 in
6 in

3) ____

12 m
8 m
6 m

4) ____

6 cm
8 cm
16 cm

5) ____

10 ft
18 ft
14 ft

6) ____

10 m
22 m
12 m

✎ *Find the surface area of each Rectangular Prism.*

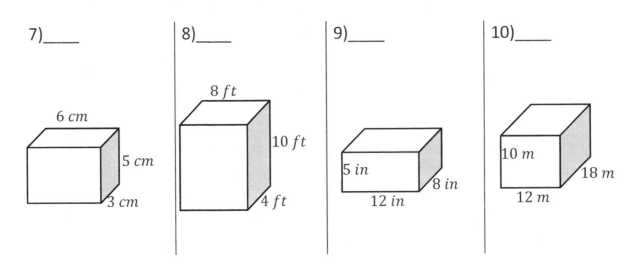

7) ____

6 cm
5 cm
3 cm

8) ____

8 ft
10 ft
4 ft

9) ____

5 in
8 in
12 in

10) ____

10 m
18 m
12 m

Cylinder

✎ *Find the volume of each Cylinder.* (π = 3.14)

1) _____

15 in   3 in

2) _____

9 cm   5 cm

3) _____

15 in   8 in

4) _____

18 ft   9 ft

5) _____

18 in   8 in

6) _____

22 in   12 in

✎ *Find the surface area of each Cylinder.* (π = 3.14)

7) _____

12 in   4 in

8) _____

9 cm   5 cm

9) _____

14 ft   6 ft

10) _____

15 m   5 m

Answers – Chapter 11

The Pythagorean Theorem

1) *no*

2) *no*

3) *no*

4) *yes*

5) *no*

6) *no*

7) *yes*

8) *yes*

9) 25

10) 12

11) 6

12) 34

13) 10

14) 5

15) 13

16) 25

Triangles

1) 7°

2) 55°

3) 43°

4) 55°

5) 45°

6) 46°

7) 52°

8) 71°

9) 27

10) 54

11) 72 cm^2

12) 72 in^2

Polygons

1) 24 cm

2) 40 m

3) 40 cm

4) 32 m

5) 96 m

6) 56 m

7) 28 cm

8) 120 ft

9) 64 ft

10) 80 in

11) 60 ft

12) 180 in

Circles

1) $37.68 \ in$

2) $62.8 \ cm$

3) $119.32 \ ft$

4) $75.36 \ m$

5) $113.04 \ cm$

6) $94.2 \ miles$

7) $119.32 \ in$

8) $138.16 \ ft$

9) $157 \ m$

10) $175.84 \ m$

11) $219.8 \ in$

12) $314 \ ft$

	Radius	Diameter	Circumference	Area
Circle 1	2 inches	4 inches	12.56 inches	12.56 square inches
Circle 2	4 meters	8 meters	25.12 meters	50.24 square meters
Circle 3	6 feet	12 feet	37.68 feet	113.04 square feet
Circle 4	8 miles	16 miles	50.24 miles	200.96 square miles
Circle 5	4.5 kilometers	9 kilometers	28.26 kilometers	63.585 square kilometers
Circle 6	7 centimeters	14 centimeters	43.96 centimeters	153.86 square centimeters
Circle 7	9 feet	18 feet	56.52 feet	254.34 square feet
Circle 8	5 meters	10 meters	31.4 meters	78.5 square meters
Circle 9	11 inches	22 inches	69.08 inches	379.94 square inches
Circle 10	10 feet	20 feet	62.8 feet	314 square feet

Cubes

1) $42.875 \ cm^3$

2) $74.088 \ cm^3$

3) $614.125 \ ft^3$

4) $1,000 \ m^3$

5) $2,197 \ in^3$

6) $614.125 \ m^3$

7) $421.875 \ km^3$

8) $274.625 \ cm^3$

9) $4,096 \ ft^3$

10) $4,913 \ mm^3$

11) $27,000 \ in^3$

12) $64,000 \ km^3$

13) $3,750 \ m^2$

14) $9,600 \ m^2$

15) $12,150 \ ft^2$

16) $21,600 \ mm^2$

17) $33,750 \ km^2$

18) $48,600 \ cm^2$

Trapezoids

1) $104\ cm^2$

2) $216\ m^2$

3) $54\ ft^2$

4) $63\ cm^2$

5) $48\ cm^2$

6) $112\ in^2$

7) $352\ cm^2$

8) $280\ in^2$

9) $7.6\ cm$

10) $16\ ft$

11) $35\ m$

12) $3\ ft$

Rectangular Prisms

1) $240\ m^3$

2) $840\ in^3$

3) $576\ m^3$

4) $768\ cm^3$

5) $2,520\ ft^3$

6) $2,640\ m^3$

7) $126\ cm^2$

8) $304\ ft^2$

9) $392\ in^2$

10) $1,032\ m^2$

Cylinder

1) $423.9\ in^3$

2) $706.5\ cm^3$

3) $3,014.4\ in^3$

4) $4,578.12\ ft^3$

5) $3,617.28\ in^3$

6) $9,947.52\ in^3$

7) $401.92\ in^2$

8) $439.6\ cm^2$

9) $753.6\ ft^2$

10) $628\ m^2$

Chapter 12: Statistics

Math Topics that you'll learn in this Chapter:

- ✓ Mean, Median, Mode, and Range of the Given Data
- ✓ Pie Graph
- ✓ Probability Problems
- ✓ Permutations and Combinations

Chapter 12: Statistics

Mean, Median, Mode, and Range of the Given Data

✎ *Find the values of the Given Data.*

1) 5, 12, 2, 2, 6

Mode: _____   Range: _____

Mean: _____   Median: _____

2) 5, 9, 3, 6, 4, 3

Mode: _____   Range: _____

Mean: _____   Median: _____

3) 12, 5, 8, 7, 8

Mode: _____   Range: _____

Mean: _____   Median: _____

4) 9, 7, 12, 7, 3, 4

Mode: _____   Range: _____

Mean: _____   Median: _____

5) 9, 7, 10, 5, 7, 4, 14

Mode: _____   Range: _____

Mean: _____   Median: _____

6) 8, 1, 6, 6, 9, 2, 17

Mode: _____   Range: _____

Mean: _____   Median: _____

7) 14, 5, 2, 7, 10, 7, 8, 13

Mode: _____   Range: _____

Mean: _____   Median: _____

8) 12, 14, 6, 4, 10, 8, 2

Mode: _____   Range: _____

Mean: _____   Median: _____

9) 17, 13, 16, 12, 14, 24

Mode: _____   Range: _____

Mean: _____   Median: _____

10) 18, 15, 10, 8, 4, 7, 8, 18

Mode: _____   Range: _____

Mean: _____   Median: _____

Pie Graph

✎*The circle graph below shows all Wilson's expenses for last month. Wilson spent* $300 *on his bills last month.*

Answer following questions based on the Pie graph.

Wilson's last month expenses

Clothes
30%

Books
10%

Others
28%

Foods
20%

Bills
12%

1) How much was Wilson's total expenses last month? _____

2) How much did Wilson spend on his clothes last month? _____

3) How much did Wilson spend for foods last month? _____

4) How much did Wilson spend on his books last month? _____

5) What fraction is Wilson's expenses for his bills and clothes out of his total

   expenses last month? _____

Chapter 12: Statistics

Probability Problems

1) If there are 15 red balls and 30 blue balls in a basket, what is the probability that Oliver will pick out a red ball from the basket? _____

Gender	Under 45	45 or older	Total
Male	12	6	18
Female	5	7	12
Total	17	13	30

2) The table above shows the distribution of age and gender for 30 employees in a company. If one employee is selected at random, what is the probability that the employee selected be either a female under age 45 or a male age 45 or older? _____

3) A number is chosen at random from 1 to 18. Find the probability of not selecting a composite number. (A composite number is a number that is divisible by itself, 1 and at least one other whole number) _____

4) There are 6 blue marbles, 8 red marbles, and 5 yellow marbles in a box. If Ava randomly selects a marble from the box, what is the probability of selecting a red or yellow marble? _____

5) A bag contains 20 balls: three green, six black, eight blue, a brown, a red and one white. If 19 balls are removed from the bag at random, what is the probability that a brown ball has been removed? _____

6) There are only red and blue marbles in a box. The probability of choosing a red marble in the box at random is one third. If there are 160 blue marbles, how many marbles are in the box? _____

Permutations and Combinations

✎ *Calculate the value of each.*

1) $5! = $ ____

2) $6! = $ ____

3) $8! = $ ____

4) $5! + 6! = $ ____

5) $8! + 3! = $ ____

6) $6! + 7! = $ ____

7) $8! + 4! = $ ____

8) $9! - 3! = $ ____

✎ *Solve each word problems.*

9) Sophia is baking cookies. She uses milk, flour and eggs. How many different orders of ingredients can she try? _____

10) William is planning for his vacation. He wants to go to restaurant, watch a movie, go to the beach, and play basketball. How many different ways of ordering are there for him? _____

11) How many 7 −digit numbers can be named using the digits $1, 2, 3, 4, 5, 6$ and 7 without repetition? _____

12) In how many ways can 9 boys be arranged in a straight line? _____

13) In how many ways can 8 athletes be arranged in a straight line? _____

14) A professor is going to arrange her 6 students in a straight line. In how many ways can she do this? _____

15) How many code symbols can be formed with the letters for the word BLUE? _____

16) In how many ways a team of 8 basketball players can choose a captain and co-captain? _____

Answers – Chapter 12

Mean, Median, Mode, and Range of the Given Data

1) Mode: 2   Range: 10   Mean: 5.4   Median: 5

2) Mode: 3   Range: 6   Mean: 5   Median: 4.5

3) Mode: 8   Range: 7   Mean: 8   Median: 8

4) Mode: 7   Range: 9   Mean: 7   Median: 7

5) Mode: 7   Range: 10   Mean: 8   Median: 7

6) Mode: 6   Range: 16   Mean: 7   Median: 6

7) Mode: 7   Range: 12   Mean: 8.25   Median: 7.5

8) Mode: *no mode*   Range: 12   Mean: 8   Median: 8

9) Mode: *no mode*   Range: 12   Mean: 16   Median: 15

10) Mode: 8,18   Range: 14   Mean: 11   Median: 9

Pie Graph

1) $2,500

2) $750

3) $500

4) $250

5) $\frac{21}{50}$

Probability Problems

1) $\frac{1}{3}$

2) $\frac{11}{30}$

3) $\frac{7}{18}$

4) $\frac{13}{19}$

5) $\frac{19}{20}$

6) 240

Permutations and Combinations

1) 120

2) 720

3) 40,320

4) 840

5) 40,326

6) 5,760

7) 40,344

8) 362,874

9) 6

10) 24

11) 5,040

12) 362,880

13) 40,320

14) 720

15) 24

16) 56

Chapter 13:
Functions Operations

Math Topics that you'll learn in this Chapter:

- ✓ Function Notation and Evaluation
- ✓ Adding and Subtracting Functions
- ✓ Multiplying and Dividing Functions
- ✓ Composition of Functions

Function Notation and Evaluation

✍ *Evaluate each function.*

1) $f(x) = x - 3$, find $f(-2)$

_____

2) $g(x) = x + 5$, find $g(6)$

_____

3) $h(x) = x + 8$, find $h(2)$

_____

4) $f(x) = -x - 7$, find $f(5)$

_____

5) $f(x) = 2x - 7$, find $f(-1)$

_____

6) $w(x) = -2 - 4x$, find $w(5)$

_____

7) $g(n) = 6n - 3$, find $g(-2)$

_____

8) $h(x) = -8x + 12$, find $h(3)$

_____

9) $k(n) = 14 - 3n$, find $k(3)$

_____

10) $g(x) = 4x - 4$, find $g(-2)$

_____

11) $k(n) = 8n - 7$, find $k(4)$

_____

12) $w(n) = -2n + 14$, find $w(5)$

_____

13) $h(x) = 5x - 18$, find $h(8)$

_____

14) $g(n) = 2n^2 + 2$, find $g(5)$

_____

15) $f(x) = 3x^2 - 13$, find $f(2)$

_____

16) $g(n) = 5n^2 + 7$, find $g(-3)$

_____

17) $h(n) = 5n^2 - 10$, find $h(4)$

_____

18) $g(x) = -3x^2 - 6x$, find $g(2)$

_____

19) $k(n) = 4n^3 + n$, find $k(-5)$

_____

20) $f(x) = -3x + 10$, find $f(3x)$

_____

21) $k(a) = 4a + 9$, find $k(a - 1)$

_____

22) $h(x) = 8x + 4$, find $h(5x)$

_____

Adding and Subtracting Functions

✍ *Perform the indicated operation.*

1) $f(x) = x + 4$

   $g(x) = 2x + 5$

   Find $(f - g)(2)$

   _____

2) $g(x) = x - 2$

   $f(x) = -x - 6$

   Find $(g - f)(-2)$

   _____

3) $h(t) = 4t + 4$

   $g(t) = 3t + 2$

   Find $(h + g)(-1)$

   _____

4) $g(a) = 5a - 7$

   $f(a) = a^2 + 3$

   Find $(g + f)(2)$

   _____

5) $g(x) = 4x - 5$

   $f(x) = 6x^2 + 5$

   Find $(g - f)(-2)$

   _____

6) $h(x) = x^2 + 3$

   $g(x) = -4x + 1$

   Find $(h + g)(4)$

   _____

7) $f(x) = -3x - 9$

   $g(x) = x^2 + 5$

   Find $(f - g)(6)$

   _____

8) $h(n) = -4n^2 + 9$

   $g(n) = 5n + 6$

   Find $(h - g)(5)$

   _____

9) $g(x) = 4x^2 - 3x - 1$

   $f(x) = 6x + 10$

   Find $(g - f)(a)$

   _____

10) $g(t) = -6t - 7$

   $f(t) = -t^2 + 3t + 15$

   Find $(g + f)(t)$

   _____

Multiplying and Dividing Functions

✍ *Perform the indicated operation.*

1) $g(x) = x + 6$

   $f(x) = x + 4$

   Find $(g.f)(2)$

   _____

2) $f(x) = 3x$

   $h(x) = -x + 5$

   Find $(f.h)(-2)$

   _____

3) $g(a) = a + 5$

   $h(a) = 2a - 4$

   Find $(g.h)(4)$

   _____

4) $f(x) = 3x + 2$

   $h(x) = 2x - 3$

   Find $(\frac{f}{h})(2)$

   _____

5) $f(x) = a^2 - 2$

   $g(x) = -4 + 3a$

   Find $(\frac{f}{g})(2)$

   _____

6) $g(a) = 4a + 6$

   $f(a) = 2a - 8$

   Find $(\frac{g}{f})(3)$

   _____

7) $g(t) = t^2 + 6$

   $h(t) = 2t - 3$

   Find $(g.h)(-3)$

   _____

8) $g(x) = x^2 + 3x + 4$

   $h(x) = 2x + 6$

   Find $(g.h)(2)$

   _____

9) $g(a) = 2a^2 - 5a + 1$

   $f(a) = 2a^3 - 6$

   Find $(\frac{g}{f})(4)$

   _____

10) $g(x) = -3x^2 + 4 - 2x$

    $f(x) = x^2 - 5$

    Find $(g.f)(3)$

    _____

Answers – Chapter 13

Function Notation and Evaluation

1) -5

2) 11

3) 10

4) -12

5) -9

6) -22

7) -15

8) -12

9) 5

10) -12

11) 25

12) 4

13) 22

14) 52

15) -1

16) 52

17) 70

18) -24

19) -505

20) $-9x + 10$

21) $4a + 5$

22) $40x + 4$

Adding and Subtracting Functions

1) -3

2) 0

3) -1

4) 10

5) -42

6) 4

7) -68

8) -122

9) $4a^2 - 9a - 11$

10) $-t^2 - 3t + 8$

Multiplying and Dividing Functions

1) 48

2) -42

3) 36

4) 8

5) 1

6) -9

7) -135

8) 140

9) $\frac{13}{122}$

10) -116

Time to Test

Time to refine your skill with a practice examination

Take a practice STAAR Math Test to simulate the test day experience. After you've finished, score your test using the answer key.

Before You Start

- You'll need a pencil and a calculator to take the test.

- There are two types of questions:

  Multiple choice questions: for each of these questions, there are four or more possible answers. Choose which one is best.

  Grid-ins questions: for these questions, write your answer in the box provided.

- It's okay to guess. You won't lose any points if you're wrong.

- The STAAR Mathematics test contains a formula sheet, which displays formulas relating to geometric measurement and certain algebra concepts. Formulas are provided to test-takers so that they may focus on application, rather than the memorization, of formulas.

- After you've finished the test, review the answer key to see where you went wrong and what areas you need to improve.

Good luck!

STAAR Grade 8 Math Practice Test 1

2023 - 2024

50 questions

Total time for this section: No time limit

You may use a calculator on this Test.

131

STAAR Grade 8 Mathematics Formula Sheet

LINEAR EQUATIONS	
Slope – intercept form	$y = mx + b$
Direct Variation	$y = kx$
Slope of a Line	$m = \dfrac{y_2 - y_1}{x_2 - x_1}$

CIRCUMFERENCE	
Circle	$C = 2\pi r$ or $C = \pi d$

AREA	
Triangle	$A = \dfrac{1}{2}bh$
Parallelogram	$A = bh$
Trapezoid	$A = \dfrac{1}{2}h(b_1 + b_2)$
Circle	$A = \pi r^2$

SURFACE AREA	Lateral	Total
Prism	$S = Ph$	$S = Ph + 2B$
Cylinder	$S = 2\pi rh$	$S = 2\pi rh + 2\pi r^2$

VOLUME	
Prism or Cylinder	$V = Bh$
Pyramid or Cone	$V = \dfrac{1}{3}Bh$
Sphere	$V = \dfrac{4}{3}\pi r^3$

ADDITIONAL INFORMATION	
Pythagorean theorem	$a^2 + b^2 = c^2$
Simple interest	$I = prt$
Compound Interest	$A = p(1 + r)^t$

1) Four one – foot rulers can be split among how many users to leave each with $\frac{1}{3}$ of a ruler?

   A. 4

   B. 6

   C. 12

   D. 24

2) If $a = 120°$ and $b = 98°$, what is the value of the c? (Figure not drawn to scale.)

   A. 19°

   B. 22°

   C. 35°

   D. 45°

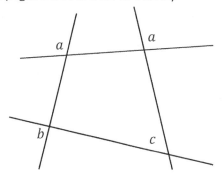

3) A rectangular concrete driveway is 25 feet long, 6 feet wide, and 24 inches thick. What is the volume of the concrete?

   A. $300\ ft^3$

   B. $660\ ft^3$

   C. $963\ ft^3$

   D. $1,800\ ft^3$

4) A pair of shoes originally priced at $45.00 was on sale for 15% off. Nick received a 20% employee discount applied to the sale price. How much did Nick pay for the shoes?

   A. $30.60

   B. $34.50

   C. $37.30

   D. $42.25

5) In a certain state, the sales tax rate increased from 8% to 8.5%. What was the increase in the sales tax on a $250 item?

   A. $1.00

   B. $1.25

   C. $1.90

   D. $2.30

6) In the xy −plane, the point $(1, 2)$ and $(−1, 6)$ are on line A. Which of the following points could also be on line A?

   A. $(−3, 2)$

   B. $(−3, 5)$

   C. $(−2, 5)$

   D. $(3, −2)$

7) In a box of blue and black marbles, the ratio of blue marbles to black marbles is $4 : 3$. If the box contains 150 black marbles, how many blue marbles are there?

   Write your answer in the box below.

8) The set of possible values of n is $\{5, 3, 7\}$. What is the set of possible values of m if $2m = n + 5$?

   A. $\{2, 4, 7\}$

   B. $\{5, 4, 6\}$

   C. $\{3, 2, 5\}$

   D. $\{4, 5, 8\}$

9) Jack scored a mean of 80 per test in his first 4 tests. In his 5th test, he scored 90. What was Jack's mean score for the 5 tests?

   A. 70

   B. 75

   C. 80

   D. 82

10) The volume of a cube is less than $64\ m^3$. Which of the following can be the cube's side?

    A. $2\ m$

    B. $4\ m$

    C. $8\ m$

    D. $11\ m$

11) $\frac{5}{8}$ of a number is 90. Find the number.

    Write your answer in the box below.

12) The following table represents the value of x and function $f(x)$. Which of the following could be the equation of the function $f(x)$?

    A. $f(x) = x^2 - 5$

    B. $f(x) = x^2 - 1$

    C. $f(x) = \sqrt{x+2}$

    D. $f(x) = \sqrt{x} + 4$

x	$f(x)$
1	5
4	6
9	7
16	8

13) What is the area of an isosceles right triangle that has one leg that measures $6\ cm$?

    A. $6\ cm^2$

    B. $12\ cm^2$

    C. $18\ cm^2$

    D. $36\ cm^2$

14) If $0.00104 = \frac{104}{x}$, what is the value of x?

    A. $1,000$

    B. $10,000$

    C. $100,000$

    D. $1,000,000$

15) A bag is filled with numbered cards from 1 to 15 and picked on at random. What is the probability that the card picked is number 8?

A. $\frac{8}{15}$

B. $\frac{7}{15}$

C. $\frac{2}{15}$

D. $\frac{1}{15}$

16) What is the value of x in the figure below?

A. $32°$

B. $46°$

C. $54°$

D. $63°$

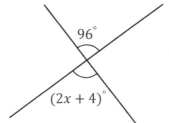

17) What is the value of the following expression? $|-5| + 9 \times 2\frac{1}{3} + (-3)^2 =$

A. 26

B. 35

C. 43

D. 51

18) How many different two-digit numbers can be formed from the digits $6, 7,$ and 5, if the numbers must be even and no digit can be repeated?

A. 1

B. 2

C. 3

D. 4

19) A juice mixture contains $\frac{5}{14}$ jar of cherry juice and $\frac{5}{70}$ jar of apple juice. How many jars of cherry juice per jar of apple juice does the mixture contain?

Write your answer in the box below.

20) If $\frac{2y}{x} - \frac{y}{3x} = \frac{(\ldots)}{3x}$ and $x \neq 0$, what expression is represented by $(\ldots)$?

   A. $2y + 4$

   B. $3y - 6$

   C. $5y$

   D. $6y$

21) Each number in a sequence is 4 more than twice the number that comes just before it. If 84 is a number in the sequence, what number comes just before it?

   A. 26

   B. 35

   C. 40

   D. 52

22) A rectangle has 14 cm wide and 5 cm length. What is the perimeter of this rectangle?

   A. 38 cm

   B. 43 cm

   C. 49 cm

   D. 58 cm

23) What is the value of the following expression? $3\frac{1}{4} + 2\frac{4}{16} + 1\frac{3}{8} + 5\frac{1}{2}$

   A. $3\frac{10}{14}$

   B. $4\frac{1}{2}$

   C. $12\frac{4}{16}$

   D. $12\frac{3}{8}$

24) A certain insect has a mass of 85 milligrams. What is the insect's mass in grams?

   A. 0.08

   B. 0.085

   C. 0.85

   D. 85

25) If $m = 6$ and $n = -3$, what is the value of $\frac{5-9(3+n)}{3m-5(2-n)} = ?$

A. $-\frac{4}{7}$

B. $-\frac{5}{7}$

C. $\frac{3}{7}$

D. $\frac{2}{7}$

26) Clara has 602 candies. She gives all her candies to her 7 friends. Each friend gets the same number of candies. How many candies will each friend get?

A. 72

B. 86

C. 89

D. 94

27) How long will it take to receive $360 in investment of $240 at the rate of 10% simple interest?

A. 9 years

B. 15 years

C. 18 years

D. 21 years

28) How many hours are there in 1,800 minutes?

A. 20 hours

B. 25 hours

C. 30 hours

D. 33 hours

29) The average of 6 numbers is 10. The average of 4 of those numbers is 7. What is the average of the other two numbers?

Write your answer in the box below.

30) The shaded sector of the circle shown below has an area of 12π square feet. What is the circumference of the circle?

A. 24π feet

B. 81π feet

C. 124π feet

D. 180π feet

31) Which of the following is a factor of 45?

A. 7

B. 9

C. 11

D. 13

32) By what percent did the price of a shirt increase if its price was increased from $15.30 to $18.36?

A. 10%

B. 12%

C. 16%

D. 20%

33) The greatest common factor of 32 and x is 8. How many possible values for x are greater than 10 and less than 60?

A. 1

B. 4

C. 6

D. 7

34) A box contains 6 strawberry candies, 4 orange candies, and 3 banana candies. If Roberto selects 2 candies at random from this box, without replacement, what is the probability that both candies are not orange?

A. $\frac{1}{8}$

B. $\frac{2}{13}$

C. $\frac{6}{13}$

D. $\frac{1}{28}$

35) $100(3 + 0.1)^2 - 100 = \cdots$

A. 861

B. 865.5

C. 1,000

D. 1,000.3

36) How many integers are between $\frac{7}{2}$ and $\frac{30}{4}$?

A. 3

B. 4

C. 6

D. 10

37) In the figure below, $LMNO$ and $JMPQ$ are squares. Point O is the center of the circle, and points L and N are on the circle. If the area of the square $LMNO$ is 16 square centimeters, what is the area, in square centimeters, of the shaded part? ($\pi = 3.14$)

Write your answer in the box below.

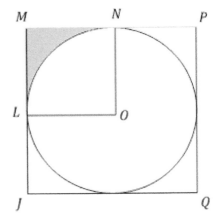

38) $(4m + 8) - (6 - 8m) =$

   A. $12m + 2$

   B. $10 + 2$

   C. $8m - 2$

   D. $6m + 2$

39) Triangle ABC is graphed on a coordinate grid with vertices at $A(-3, -2)$, $B(-1, 4)$ and $C(7, 9)$. Triangle ABC is reflected over x axes to create triangle $A'B'C'$. Which order pair represents the coordinate of C'?

   A. $(7, 9)$

   B. $(-7, -9)$

   C. $(-7, 9)$

   D. $(7, -9)$

40) Which of the following is the solution of the following inequality?

$$2x + 4 > 11x - 12.5 - 3.5x$$

   A. $x < 3$

   B. $x > 3$

   C. $x \leq 4$

   D. $x \geq 4$

41) What is the volume of the following triangular prism?

   A. $12\ m^3$

   B. $24\ m^3$

   C. $30\ m^3$

   D. $32\ m^3$

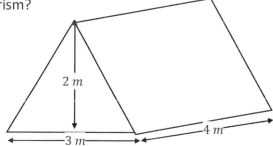

42) A student made a list of all possible products of 2 different numbers in the set below. What fraction of the products are odd?

$$\{1, 4, 6, 5, 7\}$$

A. $\dfrac{2}{5}$

B. $\dfrac{3}{10}$

C. $\dfrac{4}{15}$

D. $\dfrac{8}{17}$

43) Which of the following equations has a graph that is a straight line?

A. $y = 3x^2 + 9$

B. $x^2 + y^2 = 1$

C. $4x - 2y = 2x$

D. $7x + 2xy = 6$

44) If $5n$ is a positive even number, how many odd numbers are in the range from $5n$ up to and including $5n + 6$?

A. 2

B. 3

C. 4

D. 5

45) If $2x - 5y = 10$, what is x in terms of y?

A. $x = \dfrac{5}{2}y + 5$

B. $x = \dfrac{2}{5}y + 10$

C. $x = -\dfrac{5}{2}y - 5$

D. $x = -\dfrac{5}{2}y + 5$

46) For what value of x is the proportion true? $x: 40 = 20: 32$

    A. 16

    B. 25

    C. 28

    D. 32

47) When asked a certain question in a poll, 76% of the people polled answered yes. If 66 people did not answer yes to that question, what is the total number of people who were polled?

    A. 75

    B. 156

    C. 245

    D. 275

48) Which percentage is closest in value to 0.0099?

    A. 2%

    B. 0.1%

    C. 1%

    D. 100%

49) $\frac{6}{11}$ of a number is 96. What is the number?

    A. 97

    B. 128

    C. 154

    D. 176

50) A train travels 1,500 miles from New York to Oklahoma. The train covers the first 280 miles in 4 hours. If the train continues to travel at this rate, how many more hours will it take to reach Oklahoma City? Round your answer to the nearest whole hour.

    A. 12

    B. 15

    C. 17

    D. 20

STOP: This is the End of Test 1.

STAAR Grade 8 Math Practice Test 2

2023 - 2024

50 questions

Total time for this section: No time limit

**You may use a calculator on this Test.**

145

STAAR Grade 8 Mathematics Formula Sheet

LINEAR EQUATIONS	
Slope – intercept form	$y = mx + b$
Direct Variation	$y = kx$
Slope of a Line	$m = \dfrac{y_2 - y_1}{x_2 - x_1}$

CIRCUMFERENCE	
Circle	$C = 2\pi r$ or $C = \pi d$

AREA	
Triangle	$A = \dfrac{1}{2}bh$
Parallelogram	$A = bh$
Trapezoid	$A = \dfrac{1}{2}h(b_1 + b_2)$
Circle	$A = \pi r^2$

SURFACE AREA	Lateral	Total
Prism	$S = Ph$	$S = Ph + 2B$
Cylinder	$S = 2\pi rh$	$S = 2\pi rh + 2\pi r^2$

VOLUME	
Prism or Cylinder	$V = Bh$
Pyramid or Cone	$V = \dfrac{1}{3}Bh$
Sphere	$V = \dfrac{4}{3}\pi r^3$

ADDITIONAL INFORMATION	
Pythagorean theorem	$a^2 + b^2 = c^2$
Simple interest	$I = prt$
Compound Interest	$A = p(1 + r)^t$

1) Tomas is 6 feet 8.5 inches tall, and Alex is 5 feet 3 inches tall. What is the difference in height, in inches, between Alex and Tomas?

   A. 2.5

   B. 7.5

   C. 12.5

   D. 17.5

2) The ratio of two sides of a parallelogram is $2:3$. If its perimeter is $40\ cm$, find the length of its sides.

   A. $8\ cm, 12\ cm$

   B. $10\ cm, 14\ cm$

   C. $12\ cm, 16\ cm$

   D. $14\ cm, 18\ cm$

3) If Anna multiplies her age by 5 and then adds 3, she will get a number equal to her mother's age. If x is her mother's age, what is Anna's age in terms of x?

   A. $\dfrac{x-3}{5}$

   B. $\dfrac{x-5}{3}$

   C. $3x + 5$

   D. $5x - 3$

4) In the parallelogram below, what is the value of $x + y$?

   A. 180

   B. 230

   C. 250

   D. 360

5) If $x - 1$ is an even integer, which one of the following must be an odd integer?

   A. $2x$

   B. $2x + 1$

   C. $2x - 2$

   D. $2x + 4$

6) In a scale diagram, 0.15 inch represents 150 feet. How many inches represent 2.5 feet?

A. 0.001 in

B. 0.012 in

C. 0.0025 in

D. 0.002 in

7) Mary has 8 blue pens, 2 green pens, and 4 black pens. If she picks out one pen randomly, what is the probability that she picks a blue pen?

A. $\frac{3}{7}$

B. $\frac{4}{7}$

C. $\frac{5}{7}$

D. $\frac{6}{7}$

8) A car travels at a speed of 72 miles per hour. How far will it travel in 8 hours?

A. 574 miles

B. 576 miles

C. 578 miles

D. 580 miles

9) Which of the following numbers has factors that include the smallest factor (other than 1) of 95?

A. 28

B. 32

C. 39

D. 45

10) $\frac{4^2+3^2+(-5)^2}{(9+10-11)^2} =$

A. $\frac{25}{32}$

B. 56

C. -56

D. $-\frac{25}{32}$

11) Angle A and angle B are supplementary. The measure of angle A is 2 times the measure of angle B. What is the measure of angle A in degrees?

A. $100°$

B. $120°$

C. $140°$

D. $160°$

12) $200(3 + 0.01)^2 - 200 =$

A. 201.55

B. 361.08

C. 702.88

D. $1,612.02$

13) What is the average of the circumference of figure A and the area of figure B? ($\pi = 3$)
Write your answer in the box below.

Figure A

Figure B

14) What is the solution to $\frac{0.02}{0.25} = \frac{1.25}{x}$?

A. 0.150

B. 1.156

C. 11.565

D. 15.625

15) The least of 8 consecutive integers is m, and the greatest is n. What is the value of $\frac{m+n}{3}$ in terms of m?

A. $m + 1$

B. $2m + 8$

C. $\frac{2m+7}{3}$

D. $\frac{2m}{7}$

16) In the infinitely repeating decimal below, 1 is the first digit in the repeating pattern. What is the $68th$ digit? $\frac{1}{7} = 0.\overline{142857}$

A. 1

B. 2

C. 4

D. 7

17) Yesterday Kylie writes 10% of her homework. Today she writes another 18% of the entire homework. What fraction of the homework is left for her to write?

A. $\frac{7}{25}$

B. $\frac{4}{25}$

C. $\frac{18}{25}$

D. $\frac{10}{25}$

18) In a box of blue and yellow pens, the ratio of yellow pens to blue pens is $2:3$. If the box contains 9 blue pens, how many yellow pens are there?

A. 3

B. 4

C. 5

D. 6

19) What decimal is equivalent to $-\frac{6}{9}$?

A. $-0.\overline{5}$

B. $-0.\overline{6}$

C. $-0.\overline{65}$

D. $-0.\overline{7}$

20) How many positive even factors of 68 are greater than 26 and less than 60?

    A. 0

    B. 1

    C. 2

    D. 6

21) What is the value of x in the following equation? $|34 - 78| - x + |-12 + 20| = 36$

    Write your answer in the box below.

22) If x can be any integer, what is the greatest possible value of the expression $2 - x^2$?

    A. -1

    B. 0

    C. 3

    D. 2

23) A store has a container of handballs: 6 green, 5 blue, 8 white, and 10 yellow. If one ball is picked from the container at random, what is the probability that it will be green?

    A. $\dfrac{1}{5}$

    B. $\dfrac{6}{11}$

    C. $\dfrac{6}{29}$

    D. $\dfrac{8}{25}$

24) In the figure below, F is the midpoint of EH. Which segment has length $2y - x$ centimeters?

    A. EF

    B. GH

    C. EG

    D. FH

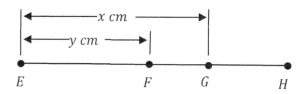

25) 12 Students had a mean score of 75. The remaining 10 students of the class had an average score of 85. What is approximately the mean (average) score of the entire class?

A. 73.5

B. 75.5

C. 77.5

D. 79.5

26) If $x = 3$, what is the approximate value of the following expression? $4x^3 + 2x + \frac{1}{x^2} + 8$

A. 112

B. 115.2

C. 122.1

D. 132.3

27) The probability of drawing a blue candy at random from a bag of 30 candies is $\frac{3}{5}$. After 6 blue candies are removed from the bag, what is the probability of randomly drawing a blue candy from the bag?

A. $\frac{1}{4}$

B. $\frac{1}{2}$

C. $\frac{3}{5}$

D. 1

28) Emma answered 9 out of 45 questions on a test incorrectly. What percentage of the questions did she answer correctly?

A. 10%

B. 40%

C. 68%

D. 80%

29) The sales price of a laptop is $1,912.50, which is 15% off the original price. What is the original price of the laptop?

Write your answer in the box below.

30) In the following parallelogram, find the value of x?

A. 40

B. 45

C. 50

D. 55

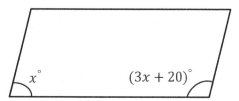

31) The reciprocal of $\frac{3}{5}$ is added to the reciprocal of $\frac{1}{4}$. What is the reciprocal of this sum?

A. $\frac{3}{5}$

B. $\frac{5}{3}$

C. $\frac{3}{17}$

D. $\frac{17}{3}$

32) Sarah walks $3\ km$ in one hour. How long does it take Sarah to walk $12\ km$ at this rate?

A. 2 hours

B. 3 hours

C. 4 hours

D. 5 hours

33) The arrow starts on space O and moves clockwise around the circle. It moves through one space each minute. What space will the arrow point to in 140 minutes?

A. O

B. P

C. Q

D. R

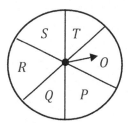

34) Evaluate: $|16 - (-5) + (-9)| - |-25|$

   A. -13

   B. 13

   C. 15

   D. -15

35) Scarlett played 5 games and had a mean score of 159. Mary played 3 games and had score of 95. What was the mean of the scores for all 8 games?

   A. 118

   B. 122

   C. 131

   D. 135

36) If $a = 3xy + 2y^2$, what is a when $x = 2$ and $y = 4$?

   A. 54

   B. 56

   C. 58

   D. 60

37) If $\sqrt{2y} = \sqrt{5x}$ then $x = \cdots$

   A. $\frac{1}{6}y$

   B. $\frac{1}{5}y$

   C. $\frac{2}{5}y$

   D. $\frac{5}{2}y$

38) For the following equation, what is the sum of the values of m when $n = 2$, when $n = 3$, and when $n = 4$? $m \times n = 66$

   A. 68.5

   B. 69.5

   C. 70.5

   D. 71.5

39) A child grows $1\frac{1}{7}$ inches in $\frac{1}{5}$ of a year. What would be his yearly growth rate in inches per year?

   A. $\frac{2}{3}$

   B. $5\frac{5}{7}$

   C. $\frac{2}{3}$

   D. $\frac{2}{3}$

40) Kim earned $55 an hour. John earned 10% less than Kim. How much money did John earn in an hour?

   A. $49.50

   B. $47.50

   C. $45.50

   D. $43.50

41) If $\left(\frac{2}{5} - \frac{1}{3}\right)x = \frac{1}{6} + \frac{2}{5}$, what is the value of x?

   Write your answer in the box below.

   ┌─────────────────────────┐
   │   │
   └─────────────────────────┘

42) Set A contains all integers from 15 to 160, inclusive, and set B contains all integers from 74 to 180, inclusive. How many integers are included in A, but not in B?

   A. 53

   B. 55

   C. 57

   D. 59

43) If 120% of a number is 60, then what is 70% of that number?

    A. 20

    B. 25

    C. 30

    D. 35

44) How many positive integers satisfy the inequality $x + 5 < 21$

    A. 10

    B. 12

    C. 14

    D. 15

45) What value of x makes the following equation true? $\frac{48}{5} = \frac{6}{x-1}$

    A. $1\frac{5}{8}$

    B. $1\frac{3}{4}$

    C. $2\frac{13}{24}$

    D. $3\frac{13}{24}$

46) $(x^6)^{\frac{7}{8}}$ is equal to ...

    A. $x^{\frac{19}{4}}$

    B. $x^{\frac{21}{4}}$

    C. $x^{\frac{23}{4}}$

    D. $x^{\frac{25}{4}}$

47) The diameter of the given semi−circular slice is 18 cm. What is the perimeter of the slice?

    $(\pi = 3.14)$

    Write your answer in the box below.

48) Find the value of x? $(2)^3 + (-3)^2 + 2x - 6 = 11$

   A. 6

   B. 4

   C. 2

   D. 0

49) Jennifer drank 2 glasses of water. There was $\frac{2}{7}$ ml of water in the first glass and $\frac{3}{8}$ ml in the second glass. How much water did Jennifer drink?

   A. $\frac{3}{4}$ ml

   B. $\frac{11}{28}$ ml

   C. $\frac{25}{56}$ ml

   D. $\frac{37}{56}$ ml

50) Four straight lines interest at point O as shown below. What is the value of x?

   A. $20°$

   B. $25°$

   C. $30°$

   D. $35°$

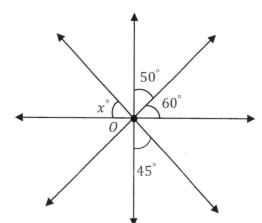

STOP: This is the End of Test 2.

STAAR Grade 8 Math Practice Tests Answer Keys

Now, it's time to review your results to see where you went wrong and what areas you need to improve.

STAAR GRADE 8 Mathematics Practice Tests Answer Key															
STAAR GRADE 8 Practice Test 1								STAAR GRADE 8 Practice Test 2							
1	C	16	B	31	B	46	B	1	D	16	C	31	C	46	B
2	B	17	B	32	D	47	D	2	A	17	C	32	C	47	46.26
3	A	18	B	33	B	48	B	3	A	18	D	33	C	48	D
4	A	19	5	34	C	49	D	4	B	19	B	34	A	49	D
5	B	20	C	35	A	50	C	5	B	20	B	35	D	50	B
6	D	21	C	36	B			6	C	21	16	36	B		
7	200	22	A	37	3.4			7	B	22	D	37	C		
8	B	23	D	38	A			8	B	23	C	38	D		
9	D	24	B	39	D			9	D	24	B	39	B		
10	A	25	B	40	A			10	A	25	D	40	A		
11	144	26	B	41	A			11	B	26	C	41	8.5		
12	D	27	B	42	B			12	D	27	B	42	D		
13	C	28	C	43	C			13	45	28	D	43	D		
14	C	29	16	44	B			14	D	29	2.25	44	D		
15	D	30	A	45	A			15	C	30	A	45	A		

STAAR Grade 8 Math Practice

Tests Answers and Explanations

STAAR GRADE 8 Mathematics Practice Test 1 Answers and Explanations

1) Choice C is correct

Divide 4 by $\frac{1}{3}$: $4 \div \frac{1}{3} = 4 \times 3 = 12$

2) Choice B is correct

The sum of all the internal angles of a simple polygon is $180(n-2)$ where n is the number of sides, so $180(4-2) = 180 \times 2 = 360$. Vertical angles are congruent. Then:

$360 = 120 + 120 + 98 + c \rightarrow c = 360 - 338 = 22$

3) Choice A is correct

First convert 24 inches to feet. 12 inch $= 1$ feet, thus: $24 \div 12 = 2$ feet. Then, calculate the volume, in cubic feet: $25 \times 6 \times 2 = 300 \ ft^3$

4) Choice A is correct

First, find the sale price. 15% of \$45.00 is \$6.75, so the sale price is $\$45.00 - \$6.75 = \$38.25$. Next, find the price after Nick's employee discount. $20\% \times \$38.25 = \$7.65$, so, the final price of the shoes is $\$38.25 - \$7.65 = \$30.60$.

5) Choice B is correct

The increase in sales tax percentage is $8.5\% - 8.0\% = 0.5\%$

0.5% of \$250 is $(0.5\%)(250) = (0.005)(250) = 1.25\$$

6) Choice D is correct

The equation of a line is in the form of $y = mx + b$, where m is the slope of the line and b is the y −intercept of the line. Two points $(1,2)$ and $(-1,6)$ are on line A. Therefore, the slope of the line A is: $m = \frac{y_2 - y_1}{x_2 - x_1} = \frac{6-2}{-1-1} = \frac{4}{-2} = -2$

The slope of line A is -2. Thus, the formula of the line A is: $y = -2x + b$, choose a point and plug in the values of x and y in the equation to solve for b. Let's choose point $(1, 2)$. Then:

$y = -2x + b \rightarrow 2 = -2(1) + b \rightarrow b = 2 + 2 = 4$

The equation of line A is: $y = -2x + 4$. So, only point $(3, -2)$ could be on the line.

7) The answer is 200

Let x be the number of blue marbles. Write the items in the ratio as a fraction:

$\frac{x}{150} = \frac{4}{3} \rightarrow 3x = 600 \rightarrow x = 200$

8) Choice B is correct

$2m = n + 5 \rightarrow m = \frac{n+5}{2}$. Substitute each value of n to find the values of m:

$m = \dfrac{5+5}{2} = \dfrac{10}{2} = 5$

$m = \dfrac{3+5}{2} = \dfrac{8}{2} = 4$

$m = \dfrac{7+5}{2} = \dfrac{12}{2} = 6$

The set of m is $\{5, 4, 6\}$

9) Choice D is correct

Jack scored a mean of 80 per test. In the first 4 tests, the sum of scores is: $80 \times 4 = 320$. Now, calculate the mean over the 5 tests: $\frac{320+90}{5} = \frac{410}{5} = 82$

10) Choice A is correct

Volume of the cube is less than $64\ m^3$. Use the formula of volume of cubes.

$\text{Volume} = (one\ side)^3 \Rightarrow 64 = (one\ side)^3$. Find the cube root of both sides.

$64 = (one\ side)^3 \rightarrow one\ side = \sqrt[3]{64} = 4$

Then: $4 = one\ side$. The side of the cube is less than 4. Only choice A is less than 4.

11) The answer is 144

Let x be the number: $\frac{5}{8}x = 90 \rightarrow x = 90 \times \frac{8}{5} = \frac{720}{5} = 144$

12) Choice D is correct

Let's review the choices when $x = 1$.

A. $f(x) = x^2 - 5$ if $x = 1 \rightarrow f(1) = (1)^2 - 5 = 1 - 5 = -4 \neq 5$

B. $f(x) = x^2 - 1$ if $x = 1 \rightarrow f(1) = (1)^2 - 1 = 1 - 1 = 0 \neq 5$

C. $f(x) = \sqrt{x+2}$ if $x = 1 \rightarrow f(1) = \sqrt{1+2} = \sqrt{3} \neq 5$

D. $f(x) = \sqrt{x} + 4$ if $x = 1 \rightarrow f(1) = \sqrt{1} + 4 = 5$

Only choice D provides a correct answer.

13) Choice C is correct

First draw an isosceles triangle. Remember that two legs of the triangle are equal.

Let put a for the legs. Then:

$a = 6 \Rightarrow$ Area of the triangle is $= \frac{1}{2}(6 \times 6) = \frac{36}{2} = 18 \ cm^2$

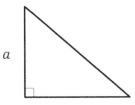

14) Choice C is correct

Solve for x: $0.00104 = \frac{104}{x}$, multiply both sides by x, $(0.00104)(x) = \frac{104}{x}(x)$.

Simplify: $0.00104x = 104$. Divide both side by 0.00104: $\frac{0.00104x}{0.00104} = \frac{104}{0.00104}$, simplify

$$x = \frac{104}{0.00104} = 100,000$$

15) Choice D is correct

The number of cards in the bag is 15. Probability $= \frac{number\ of\ desired\ outcomes}{number\ of\ total\ outcomes} = \frac{1}{15}$

16) Choice B is correct

$(2x + 4)°$ and $96°$ are vertical angles. Vertical angles are equal in measure. Then:

$2x + 4 = 96 \rightarrow 2x = 92 \rightarrow x = 46°$

17) Choice B is correct

First calculate square of -3: $|-5| + 9 \times 2\frac{1}{3} + 9$

Convert mix number to fraction, then multiply to 9: $|-5| + \frac{63}{3} + 9$

Calculate absolute value and add terms: $5 + 21 + 9 = 35$

18) Choice B is correct

The two-digit numbers must be even, so the only possible two-digit numbers must end in 6, since 6 is the only even digit given in the problem. Since the numbers cannot be repeated, the only possibilities for two-digit even numbers are 76 and 56. Thus, the answer is two possible two-digit numbers.

19) The answer is 5

Set up a proportion to solve: $\frac{\frac{5}{14}\,cherry}{\frac{5}{70}\,apple} = \frac{x\,cherry}{1\,apple} \rightarrow \frac{5}{14} \times \frac{70}{5} = x \rightarrow x = \frac{70}{14} = \frac{10}{2} \rightarrow x = 5$

20) Choice C is correct

Use properties of equations to determine the missing expression. $\frac{2y}{x} - \frac{y}{3x} = \frac{(...)}{3x}$

$\frac{3}{3} \cdot \frac{2y}{x} - \frac{y}{3x} = \frac{(...)}{3x} \rightarrow \frac{6y}{3x} - \frac{y}{3x} = \frac{(...)}{3x} \rightarrow \frac{6y - y}{3x} = \frac{(...)}{3x} \rightarrow (...) = 5y$

21) Choice C is correct

Let n represent a number in the sequence, and let x represent the number that comes just before n.

$n = 4 + 2x \rightarrow 84 = 4 + 2x \rightarrow 80 = 2x \rightarrow x = 40$

22) Choice A is correct

Perimeter of rectangle is equal to the sum of all the sides of the rectangle:

Perimeter $= 2(14) + 2(5) = 28 + 10 = 38\ cm$

23) Choice D is correct

$3\frac{1}{4} + 2\frac{4}{16} + 1\frac{3}{8} + 5\frac{1}{2}$

Convert all the fractions to a common denominator (16):

$3\frac{4}{16} + 2\frac{4}{16} + 1\frac{6}{16} + 5\frac{8}{16} = (3 + 2 + 1 + 5) + \left(\frac{4+4+6+8}{16}\right) = 11 + 1\frac{6}{16} = 12\frac{6}{16} = 12\frac{3}{8}$

24) Choice B is correct

One gram is equal to 1,000 milligrams, or 1 milligram is equal to $\frac{1}{1,000}$ gram

Thus, 85 milligrams $= \frac{85}{1,000} = 0.085$ gram

25) Choice B is correct

Substitute 6 for m and -3 for n:

$\frac{5-9(3+n)}{3m-5(2-n)} = \frac{5-9(3+(-3))}{3(6)-5(2-(-3))} = \frac{5-9(0)}{18-5(5)} = \frac{5}{18-25} = \frac{5}{-7} = -\frac{5}{7}$

26) Choice B is correct

To answer this question, we need to divide 602 by 7: $\frac{602}{7} = 86$

27) Choice B is correct

Simple interest (y) is calculated by multiplying the initial deposit (p), by the interest rate (r), and time (t). $360 = 240 \times 0.10 \times t \rightarrow 360 = 24t \rightarrow t = \frac{360}{24} = 15$

So, it takes 15 years to get $360 with an investment of $240.

28) Choice C is correct

There are 60 minutes in 1 hours. Divide the number of minutes by the number of minutes in 1

hour: $\frac{1,800}{60} = 30$ hours

29) The answer is 16

average $= \frac{sum\ of\ terms}{number\ of\ terms} \Rightarrow$ (average of 6 numbers) $10 = \frac{sum\ of\ numbers}{6}$

$\Rightarrow$ sum of 6 numbers is: $10 \times 6 = 60$

(Average of 4 numbers) $7 = \frac{sum\ of\ numbers}{4} \rightarrow$ sum of 4 numbers is $7 \times 4 = 28$

Sum of 6 numbers $-$ sum of 4 numbers $=$ sum of 2 numbers

$60 - 28 = 32$. Average of 2 numbers $= \frac{32}{2} = 16$

30) Choice A is correct

The area of the entire circle is πr^2. The fraction of the circle that is shaded is $\frac{30}{360} = \frac{1}{12}$. So, the

area of the sector is $\frac{1}{12}\pi r^2$. Use that information to find r.

$\frac{1}{12}\pi r^2 = 12\pi \rightarrow r^2 = 144 \rightarrow r = 12$

Use r to calculate the circumference of the circle: $c = 2\pi r = 2\pi(12) = 24\pi$

The circumference is 24π feet.

31) Choice B is correct

The factors of 45 are: $\{ 1, 3, 5, 9, 15, 45 \}$. Only choice B is correct.

32) Choice D is correct.

$Percent\ of\ change = \frac{new\ number - original\ number}{original\ number} = \frac{18.36 - 15.30}{15.30} = 20\%$

33) Choice B is correct

First find the multiples of 8 that fall between 10 and 60: $16, 24, 32, 40, 48, 56$. Since the

greatest common factor of 32 and x is 8, x cannot be 32 (otherwise the GCF would be 32, not

8). There are 5 remaining values: $16, 24, 40, 48$ and 56. Number 16 is also not possible (otherwise the GCF would be 16, not 8). Then, there are 4 possible values for x.

34) Choice C is correct

The total number of candies in the box is $6 + 4 + 3 = 13$. The number of candies that are not orange is $6 + 3 = 9$. The probability of the first candy not being orange is $\frac{9}{13}$. Now, out of 12 candies, there are 8 candies left that are not orange. The probability of the second candy not being orange is $\frac{8}{12}$. Multiply these two probabilities to get the solution: $\frac{9}{13} \times \frac{8}{12} = \frac{72}{156} = \frac{24}{52} = \frac{6}{13}$

35) Choice A is correct

First calculate exponents value.

$100(3 + 0.1)^2 - 100 = 100(3.1)^2 - 100 = 100(9.61) - 100 = 961 - 100 = 861$

36) Choice B is correct

First, change the improper fractions into mixed numbers: $\frac{7}{2} = 3\frac{1}{2}$ and $\frac{30}{4} = 7\frac{1}{2}$

The integers between these two values are $4, 5, 6$ and 7. So, there are 4 integers between $\frac{7}{5}$ and $\frac{30}{4}$.

37) The answer is 3.44

The area of square $LMNO$ is 16 square centimeters. So: $S^2 = 16 \rightarrow \sqrt{S^2} = \sqrt{16} \rightarrow S = 4\ cm$

Sides LO and NO are each a radius of the circle. So, the radius of the circle is $4\ cm$.

calculate the area of $\frac{1}{4}$ of the circle. The area of a circle is $A = \pi r^2$. So the area of the $\frac{1}{4}$ of the circle, in square centimeters, is $\frac{1}{4}A = \frac{1}{4}\pi r^2 = \frac{1}{4}\pi(4)^2 = \frac{1}{4}\pi(16) = 4\pi$. For calculating the area of shaded region, subtract area of $\frac{1}{4}$ of the circle from area of square.

The area of the shaded par: $16 - 4\pi$: and $\pi = 3.14$, then, the answer is:

$16 - 4\pi = 16 - 12.56 = 3.44$

38) Choice A is correct

Combine like terms: $4m + 8m - 6 + 8 \rightarrow 12m + 2$

39) Choice D is correct

When a point is reflected over x axes, the (y) coordinate of that point changes to $(-y)$ while its x coordinate remains the same. $C(7,9) \rightarrow C'(7,-9)$

40) Choice A is correct

$2x + 4 > 11x - 12.5 - 3.5x \rightarrow$ Combine like terms: $2x + 4 > 7.5x - 12.5 \rightarrow$ Subtract $2x$ from both sides: $4 > 5.5x - 12.5$. Add 12.5 both sides of the inequality. $16.5 > 5.5x$, Divide both sides by $5.5 \rightarrow \frac{16.5}{5.5} > x \rightarrow x < 3$

41) Choice A is correct

Use the volume of the triangular prism formula.

$V = \frac{1}{2}(length)(base)(high) \rightarrow V = \frac{1}{2} \times 4 \times 3 \times 2 \Rightarrow V = 12\ m^3$

42) Choice B is correct

First, list the products:

$1 \times 4 = 4$

$1 \times 6 = 6$

$1 \times 5 = 5$

$1 \times 7 = 7$

$4 \times 6 = 24$

$4 \times 5 = 20$

$4 \times 7 = 28$

$6 \times 5 = 30$

$6 \times 7 = 42$

$5 \times 7 = 35$

Out of 10 results, 3 numbers are odd. The answer is: $\frac{3}{10}$

43) Choice C is correct

Standard form of straight-line equation is: $y = mx + b$. Thus, choice C has a graph that is a straight line. All other options are not equations of straight lines.

44) Choice B is correct

Since $5n$ is even, then $5n + 1$ must be odd. Thus $5n + 3$ and $5n + 5$ are also odd. So, there are a total of 3 numbers in this range that are odd.

45) Choice A is correct

Solve for x: $2x - 5y = 10 \rightarrow x - \frac{5}{2}y = 5 \rightarrow x = \frac{5}{2}y + 5$

46) Choice B is correct

Write the ratios in fraction form and solve for x: $\frac{x}{40} = \frac{20}{32}$

Cross multiply: $32x = 800$. Apply the multiplicative inverse property; divide both sides by 32: $x = \frac{800}{32} = 25$

47) Choice D is correct

76% of the people polled answered yes, so 24% of the people did not answer yes. Therefore, 66 people is 24% of the total, x.

$\frac{66}{x} = \frac{24}{100} \rightarrow \frac{66}{x} = \frac{6}{25} \rightarrow 66(25) = 6x \rightarrow \frac{66(25)}{6} = x \rightarrow x = 275$

48) Choice B is correct

Since 0.0099 is equal to 0.99%, the closest to that value is 0.1%.

49) Choice D is correct

Let x be the number: $\frac{6}{11}x = 96 \rightarrow x = 96 \times \frac{11}{6} = 176$

50) Choice C is correct

First, find the speed of the train in miles per hour: $280 \div 4 = 70$ miles per hour

The number of miles left to travel is: $1,500 - 280 = 1,220$ miles

To find the number of hours left, use the equation

$d = rt \rightarrow (distance) = (rate) \times (time) \rightarrow 1,220 = 70t$

$t = \frac{1,220}{70} = 17.4285714$ hours. That number rounded to the nearest whole hour is 17 hours.

STAAR GRADE 8 Mathematics Practice Test 2 Answers and Explanations

1) Choice D is correct

First, convert their heights from feet and inches to inches, by multiplying the number of feet by 12 and adding the inches. Tomas: 6 feet +8.5 inches. 6(12 inches) +8.5 inches= 72 inches +8.5 inches $= 80.5$ inches. Alex: 5 feet +3 inches. 5(12 inches)+3 inches $= 60$ inches + 3 inches $= 63$ inches

Then, subtract Alex's height from Tomas's height: $80.5 - 63 = 17.5$

2) Choice A is correct

Let the lengths of two sides of the parallelogram be $2x \ cm$ and $3x \ cm$ respectively. Then, its perimeter $= 2(2x + 3x) = 10x$

Therefore, $10x = 40 \rightarrow x = 4$

One side $= 2(4) = 8 \ cm$ and other side is: $3(4) = 12 \ cm$

3) Choice A is correct

Let y be Anna's age:

$5y + 3 = x \rightarrow 5y = x - 3 \rightarrow y = \frac{x-3}{5}$

4) Choice B is correct

In a parallelogram, opposite angles are congruent. The measure of the unmarked angle is $65°$. The sum of the interior angles of a parallelogram is equal to $360°$. Use that information to solve the problem: $x + y + 65 + 65 = 360 \rightarrow x + y + 130 = 360 \rightarrow x + y = 230$

5) Choice B is correct

One more than an even integer must be odd.

One more than $x - 1$ is x, therefore x must be odd. Two times an odd integer must be even, therefore $2x$ is even. An even integer increases by 1 must be odd.

Therefore, $2x + 1$ must be odd. Choices C and D are even integers.

6) Choice C is correct

Let x be the number of inches representing 2.5 feet. Set up a proportion and solve for x:

$\frac{x}{2.5} = \frac{0.15}{150} \rightarrow x = \frac{0.15 \times 2.5}{150} \rightarrow x = 0.0025 \ in$

7) Choice B is correct

The number of pens is 14. The probability of picking a blue pen is: $\frac{8}{14} = \frac{4}{7}$

8) Choice B is correct

To answer this question, multiply 72 miles per hour to $8 \rightarrow 72 \times 8 = 576$ miles

9) Choice D is correct

To find the smallest factor of 95, list the factors: $1, 5, 19,$ and 95. The smallest factor (other than 1) is 5. Of the choices listed $(28, 32, 39,$ and $45)$, only 45 is a multiple of 5.

10) Choice A is correct

Adding exponents is done by calculating each exponent first and then adding and dividing:

$$\frac{4^2 + 3^2 + (-5)^2}{(9 + 10 - 11)^2} = \frac{16 + 9 + 25}{(8)^2} = \frac{50}{64} = \frac{25}{32}$$

11) Choice B is correct

Angle A and angle B are supplementary, so the sum of their angles is $180°$.

Let a equal the measure of angle A, and let b equal the measure of angle B.

$a + b = 180$

The measure of angle A is 2 times the measure of angle B.

$$a = 2b \rightarrow 2b + b = 180 \rightarrow 3b = 180 \rightarrow b = \frac{180}{3} = 60$$

$a = 2b = 2(60) = 120$

Therefore, the measure of angle A is $120°$.

12) Choice D is correct

First calculate exponents value, then multiplying and subtracting:

$200(3 + 0.01)^2 - 200 = 200(3.01)^2 - 200 = 200(9.06) - 200 = 1,612.02$

13) The answer is 45

Perimeter of figure A is: $2\pi r = 2\pi \frac{10}{2} = 10\pi = 10 \times 3 = 30$

Area of figure B is: $6 \times 10 = 60$, Average $= \frac{30 + 60}{2} = \frac{90}{2} = 45$

14) Choice D is correct

To eliminate the decimals in this equation, multiply the numerators and denominators by 100:

$$\left(\frac{0.02}{0.25}\right)\left(\frac{100}{100}\right) = \left(\frac{1.25}{x}\right)\left(\frac{100}{100}\right) \rightarrow \left(\frac{2}{25}\right) = \frac{125}{100x} \rightarrow x = \left(\frac{125}{100}\right)\left(\frac{25}{2}\right) = 15.625$$

15) Choice C is correct

The first integer is m, so the second is $m + 1$, the rest are $m + 2, m + 3, m + 4, m + 5, m + 6$ and finally $m + 7$. Since n is the eight and greatest of the integers, $n = m + 7$.

Substitute $m + 7$ for n and simplify: $\frac{m+n}{3} = \frac{m+m+7}{3} = \frac{2m+7}{3}$

16) Choice C is correct

There are 6 digits in the repeating decimal (0.142857), so digit 1 would be the first, seventh, thirteenth digit and so on. To find the 68th digit, divide 68 by 6.

$68 \div 6 = 11r2$

Since the remainder is 2, that means the 68th digit is the same as the 2^{ed} digit, which is 4.

17) Choice C is correct

So far, Kylie has written $10\% + 18\% = 28\%$ of the entire homework. That means she has

$100\% - 28\% = 72\%$ left to write. $72\% = \frac{72}{100} = \frac{18}{25}$

18) Choice D is correct

Let x be the number of yellow pens. Write a proportion and solve: $\frac{yellow}{blue} = \frac{2}{3} = \frac{x}{9}$

Solve the equation: $18 = 3x \rightarrow x = 6$

19) Choice B is correct

To find the decimal equivalent to $-\frac{6}{9}$, divide 6 by 9. Then:

$$-\frac{6}{9} = -0.66666\ldots = -0.\overline{6}$$

20) Choice B is correct

List the factors of 68: 1 and 68, 2 and 34, 4 and 17. There is one factor greater than 26 and less than 60.

21) The answer is 16

First calculate absolute values: $|-44| - x + |8| = 36 \rightarrow 44 - x + 8 = 36$

Combine like terms: $44 + 8 - 36 = x \rightarrow x = 16$

22) Choice D is correct

To answer this question, assign several positive and negative values to x and determine what the value of the expression will be:

x	-2	-1	0	1	2
$2 - x^2$	-2	1	2	1	-2

So, the maximum value of the expression is 2.

23) Choice C is correct

The total number of handballs in the container is $6 + 5 + 8 + 10 = 29$. Since there are 6 green handballs, the probability of selecting a green handball is $\frac{6}{29}$.

24) Choice B is correct

These facts are given: F is the midpoint of EH.

EG has a length of x cm. EF has a length of y cm.

Use the first two facts to determine that E has a length of $2y$ centimeters:

$$GH = EH - EG = 2y - x$$

25) Choice D is correct

Total score of first 12 students $= 12 \times 75 = 900$

Total score of remaining 10 students $= 10 \times 85 = 850$

Mean score of the whole class $= \frac{900+850}{22} \approx 79.5$

26) Choice C is correct

Substitute 3 for x:

$$4(3^3) + 2(3) + \frac{1}{(3)^2} + 8 = 108 + 6 + \frac{1}{9} + 8 = 122 + \frac{1}{9} = \frac{1,099}{9} \approx 122.1$$

27) Choice B is correct

Start with a proportion to determine the total number of blue candies in the bag.

$$\frac{3}{5} = \frac{r}{30} \rightarrow \frac{3}{5}(30) = r \rightarrow r = 18$$

There are currently 18 blue candies out of 30 candies in the bag. After 6 blue candies are removed, there would be 12 blue candies left in the bag and 24 total candies.

The probability of randomly drawing a blue candy would then be $\frac{12}{24} = \frac{1}{2}$

28) Choice D is correct

If Emma answered 9 out of 45 questions incorrectly, then she answered 36 questions correctly.

$\frac{36}{45} \times 100 = 80\%$

29) The answer is 2,250

Let x be the original price. Then:

$\$1,912.50 = x - 0.15(x) \rightarrow 1,912.50 = 0.85x \rightarrow x = \dfrac{1,912.50}{0.85} \rightarrow x = 2,250$

30) Choice A is correct

In a parallelogram, consecutive angles are supplementary. Thus,

$x + (3x + 20) = 180 \rightarrow 4x + 20 = 180 \rightarrow 4x = 160 \rightarrow x = 40$

31) Choice C is correct

The reciprocal of $\frac{3}{5}$ is added to the reciprocal of $\frac{1}{4}$:

$\frac{4}{1} + \frac{5}{3} = \frac{12}{3} + \frac{5}{3} = \frac{17}{3}$. The reciprocal of this sum is $\frac{3}{17}$.

32) Choice C is correct

To answer this question, divide $12\ km$ by $3\ km$ per hour: $\frac{12}{3} = 4$ hours

33) Choice C is correct

There are 6 spaces, so first divide 140 by 6: $140 \div 6 = 23$ remainder 2. So, the arrow goes around 23 full circle and then 2 more spaces. Two spaces from Space O is Space Q.

34) Choice A is correct

$|16 - (-5) + (-9)| - |-25|$

Simplify negatives inside the first absolute value brackets: $|16 + 5 - 9| - |-25|$

Simplify the first absolute value: $|12| - |-25|$. Calculate the absolute values: $12 - 25$

Perform the final subtraction: $12 - 25 = -13$

35) Choice D is correct

The sum of the scores of Scarlett's 5 games is $5(159) = 795$. The sum of the scores of Marys' 3 games is $3(95) = 285$. Add those two sums and divide by 8 to find the mean:

$\frac{795 + 285}{8} = \frac{1,080}{8} = 135$

36) Choice B is correct

Substitute 2 for x and 4 for y in the equation: $3(2)(4) + 2(4)^2 = 24 + 32 = 56$

37) Choice C is correct

Square both sides of the equation: $(\sqrt{2y})^2 = (\sqrt{5x})^2 \rightarrow 2y = 5x$

Solve for x: $x = \frac{2}{5}y$

38) Choice D is correct

First, find the value of m for each value of n.

For $n = 2$: $2m = 66 \rightarrow m = 33$

For $n = 3$: $3m = 66 \rightarrow m = 22$

For $n = 4$: $4m = 66 \rightarrow m = 16.5$

Then, add those three values together: $33 + 22 + 16.5 = 71.5$

39) Choice B is correct

Set up a proportion to solve.

$$\frac{1\frac{1}{7}\,in}{\frac{1}{5}\,yr} = \frac{x\,in}{1\,yr} \rightarrow 1\frac{1}{7} = \frac{1}{5}x \rightarrow \frac{8}{7} = \frac{1}{5}x \rightarrow \left(\frac{5}{1}\right)\left(\frac{8}{7}\right) = x \rightarrow \frac{40}{7} = x \rightarrow x = 5\frac{5}{7}$$

40) Choice A is correct

If Kim's earning $= 100\%$, then, John's earning is 90% of Kim's earning. Then:

$0.90 \times 55 = 49.50$

41) The answer is $x = 8\frac{1}{2}$ or 8.5

$$\left(\frac{2}{5} - \frac{1}{3}\right)x = \frac{1}{6} + \frac{2}{5}$$

Rewrite with equivalent fractions with like denominators.

$$\left(\frac{2\times 3}{5\times 3} - \frac{1\times 5}{3\times 5}\right)x = \frac{1\times 5}{6\times 5} + \frac{2\times 6}{5\times 6} \rightarrow \left(\frac{6}{15} - \frac{5}{15}\right)x = \frac{5}{30} + \frac{12}{30} \rightarrow \left(\frac{1}{15}\right)x = \frac{17}{30}$$

Multiply both sides of the equation by 15.

$$15\left(\frac{1}{15}\right)x = 15\left(\frac{17}{30}\right) \rightarrow x = \frac{17}{2} = 8\frac{1}{2} = 8.5$$

42) Choice D is correct

The integers that are included in Set A but not in Set B are 15 through 73. (Note that 74 is included in Set B). To calculate the number of integers between 15 and 73, inclusive, subtract the two endpoints and add 1. (One must be added because the endpoints are both counted in the total) $73 - 15 + 1 = 59$

43) Choice D is correct

Let x be the number then set the equation: $\frac{120}{100}x = 60 \rightarrow x = 60 \times \frac{100}{120} = 50$

70% of 50 is $\frac{70}{100} \times 50 = 35$

44) Choice D is correct

First, simplify the inequality: $x + 5 < 21 \rightarrow x < 16$

The positive integers that satisfy the inequality are $1, 2, 3, \ldots, 14, 15$. (We cannot include 16 because x must be less than 16) 15 positive integers satisfy this inequality.

45) Choice A is correct

$\frac{48}{5} = \frac{6}{x-1}$. Cross multiply: $48(x - 1) = 6(5)$ apply multiplicative inverse property; divide both

sides of the equation by 48. Then, simplify the fraction: $x - 1 = \frac{30}{48} \rightarrow x = \frac{30}{48} + 1 = \frac{78}{48} \rightarrow$

$x = 1\frac{30}{48} = 1\frac{5}{8}$

46) Choice B is correct

Multiply two exponents: $(x^6)^{\frac{7}{8}} = x^{6 \times \frac{7}{8}} = x^{\frac{42}{8}} = x^{\frac{21}{4}}$

47) The answer is $46.26 \ cm$

Given diameter $= 18 \ cm \rightarrow$ radius $= 9cm$

Perimeter of circle $= 2\pi r = 2 \times \pi \times 9 = 18\pi = 56.52 \ cm$

The perimeter of semi$-$circular slice is: $P = \frac{perimeter \ of \ circle}{2} + 2r = \frac{56.52}{2} + 2(9) = 46.26 \ cm$

48) Choice D is correct

$(2)^3 + (-3)^2 + 2x - 6 = 11 \rightarrow 8 + 9 + 2x - 6 = 11$

Combine like terms: $11 + 2x = 11 \rightarrow 2x = 0 \rightarrow x = 0$

49) Choice D is correct

To answer this question, add $\frac{2}{7}$ and $\frac{3}{8}$: $\frac{2}{7} + \frac{3}{8} = \frac{16+21}{56} = \frac{37}{56} \ ml$

50) Choice B is correct

Call the missing angle in the top half of the figure y. The sum of the four angles on the top of the figure is equal to $180°$: $x + y + 50 + 60 = 180$

Since y is a vertical angle with the $45°$ angle, then y is also 45°. Use that to solve for x.

$45 + x + 50 + 60 = 180 \rightarrow 155 + x = 180 \rightarrow x = 25°$

... So Much More Online!

Effortless Math Online STAAR Grade 8 Math Center offers a complete study program, including the following:

✓ Step-by-step instructions on how to prepare for the STAAR Grade 8 Math test

✓ Numerous STAAR Grade 8 Math worksheets to help you measure your math skills

✓ Complete list of STAAR Grade 8 Math formulas

✓ Video lessons for STAAR Grade 8 Math topics

✓ Full-length STAAR Grade 8 Math practice tests

✓ And much more...

No Registration Required.

Receive the PDF version of this book or get another FREE book!

Thank you for using our Book!

Do you LOVE this book?

Then, you can get the PDF version of this book or another book absolutely FREE!

Please email us at:

info@EffortlessMath.com

for details.

Author's Final Note

I hope you enjoyed reading this book. You've made it through the book! Great job!

First of all, thank you for purchasing this practice book. I know you could have picked any number of books to help you prepare for your STAAR Grade 8 Math test, but you picked this book and for that I am extremely grateful.

It took me years to write this workbook for the STAAR Grade 8 Math because I wanted to prepare a comprehensive STAAR workbook to help test takers make the most effective use of their valuable time while preparing for the test.

After teaching and tutoring math courses for over a decade, I've gathered my personal notes and lessons to develop this practice book. It is my greatest hope that the exercises in this book could help you prepare for your test successfully.

If you have any questions, please contact me at reza@effortlessmath.com and I will be glad to assist. Your feedback will help me to greatly improve the quality of my books in the future and make this book even better. Furthermore, I expect that I have made a few minor errors somewhere in this book. If you think this to be the case, please let me know so I can fix the issue as soon as possible.

If you enjoyed this book and found some benefit in reading this, I'd like to hear from you and hope that you could take a quick minute to post a review on the book's Amazon page. To leave your valuable feedback, please visit: amzn.to/3tDorFC

Or scan this QR code.

I personally go over every single review, to make sure my books really are reaching out and helping students and test takers. Please help me help STAAR Grade 8 Math test takers, by leaving a review!

I wish you all the best in your future success!

Reza Nazari

Math teacher and author

Made in the USA
Coppell, TX
04 April 2023

15182308R00116